EVERYTHING I LEARNED

AT

$200,000 MBA

ABOUT

LEADERSHIP

EVERYTHING I LEARNED

AT

$200,000 MBA

ABOUT

LEADERSHIP

RITESH PREMCHAND CHAUBE

MBA, KELLOG SCHOOL OF MANAGEMENT
NORTHWESTERN UNIVERSITY

Copyright © 2019 Ritesh Chaube

Stanfis LLC DBA 200kMBA
All rights reserved.

No part of this publication may be reproduced, distributed, or transmitted in any form or by any means, including photocopying, recording, or other electronic or mechanical methods, without the prior written permission of the copyright owners, except in the case of brief quotations embodied in critical reviews and certain other noncommercial uses permitted by copyright law.

ISBN: 9781733288903

More info at: www.200kMBA.com/Leadership

Dedicated to our Soldiers

Dedicated to the Family.

Dedicated to my readers everywhere.
Who persevere and never stop learning.

AUTHOR'S NOTE

Companies and brands mentioned in this book are not affiliated with Stanfis LLC DBA 200KMBA. I do not work for, invest in, or get paid by any of these companies. The material mentioned here is based on learnings and recollection and constitutes opinions in many cases. Readers are advised to seek information from this book, but they should ultimately make the informed choice on how they should manage their business.

TABLE OF CONTENTS

OWNERS CLUB ix

PREFACE xi

CHAPTER ONE
VISIONARY LEADERSHIP 1

CHAPTER TWO
LEADERSHIP IN ACTION 22

CHAPTER THREE
LEADING NEGOTIATIONS 51

CHAPTER FOUR
NEGOTIATING LIKE A HOSTAGE NEGOTIATOR 74

CHAPTER FIVE
LEADING IN CRISIS 92

CHAPTER SIX
LEADERSHIP IN CORPORATE GOVERNANCE 114

CHAPTER SEVEN
MASTERING LEGAL QUAGMIRE: BUSINESS LAW 123

APPENDIX 144

ABOUT MYSELF 156

TELL ME HOW I DID 157

IN CLOSING 158

OWNERS CLUB

Hello,

As Author of the $200,000 MBA series, I want to personally welcome you to the owners club. You could have bought a cheaper book on this topic, but you didn't. You chose to pay the extra money to own and learn from the finest material on the market. I certainly have admiration for your taste and appreciation for finer things in life.

As a way of saying thanks, I would like to offer you a free electronic copy of my next book on Finance when it comes out (The book on finance is gonna be a fantastic and, as always unlike anything else currently in the market). Simply join the owners club so that I can let you know:

Two ways to join (Be sure to mention your club code LEADER200K)

Email: rc@200kMBA.com

Or

Visit: 200kMBA.com/OwnersClub

P.S.: If you also want a hard copy, just email me and I'll get you one.

x

PREFACE

The brave may not live forever, but the cautious don't live at all.

\- Richard Branson, Founder, Virgin Group

If my family and friends could read just one book about Leadership, which book would that be? That is the goal I had in mind. I wrote this book for them and now I am sharing this book with you. With hostage negotiators, cyanide in Tylenol bottles, and needle syringes in Pepsi, this is a leadership book that reads like a thriller.

Hello, my name is Ritesh and this book will share everything amazing I learned at the **#1 Business School in the World for Marketing**: Kellogg School of Management. Top MBA programs are pretty pricey. Sticker price: $200k. If you can afford it, it is worth it. Otherwise, this book is the closest substitute. Read on. I promise not to take myself too seriously.

Unlike most boring MBA books out there, this book is fun. Like watching episodes of "MBA Professors Gone Wild". This book pretends that we are all adults here and uses a relaxed language. Full of day-to-day conversational terms like "shitty," "sucks," and "blows" to keep you entertained and awake.

We will cover everything from vision formulation and principles of global leadership to negotiating like FBI hostage negotiators, managing crisis with calm, effective corporate governance, lobbying and effecting change of regulation by mastering the legal system. From Steve Jobs to

Richard Branson, we examine how well they stacked up on the leadership scale.

Almost everything in MBA is full of rabbit holes. Or like water caves. You go down one of these and by the time you come back up, 50 years have passed by. And you find that are not even halfway done with the material. That's because MBA professors, and academics in general, like to write long winding books about concepts, which, in essence, are very simple and can be laid out in a few paragraphs.

So, the trick is to learn about topics in just enough depth so that you know enough to make informed decisions. Or contribute to management meetings. Or, not look like a deer-in-the-headlights when a whale-sized customer talks about some MBA concept like 'marginal pricing'. You can always go back and delve deeper into the topic, if the need arises. At least, you know what to look for and which rabbit hole to go down to. We will steer clear of rabbit holes and explore fascinating facts that tie into business lessons.

HOW IS THIS BOOK DIFFERENT?

This book will unleash a visionary approach to leadership using everything I have learned through continued education, research, and years of professional experience.

What makes this book good is that I regularly put my $200k ego aside and am willing to learn from the experts in the field. No matter who they are. I go out and seek the best knowledge on the subject from the real gurus, whether they have an MBA or PhD or not. Whether academia has celebrated them or not. And, that makes everything I write simply the best in the field. For example, one of the experts I learned negotiations from is Chris Voss. He used to be a FBI hostage negotiator.

It is kinda cool that most professors who taught us are experts in the field. But, professors can be weird on some issues. They get mind-fucked because they are surrounded by so much academic shit. So, if they don't make sense on a certain topic, I openly disagree with then and look for better explanations elsewhere. Accordingly, this book presents a combination of knowledge you won't find anywhere. Period. In every topic covered in this book, I have made the effort to push the science forward and make it accessible to everyone. To provide the depth of information with the ease of understanding that is uncommon among business books. For every concept in this book, I followed these steps:

- Look at the latest research on the topic.
- Look at the industry best practice.
- Remove waste theoretical.
- Remove complicated academic jargon.
- Simplify the language.
- Make it easier to understand.
- Illustrate with fascinating facts and real examples.
- Serve it all with a side of humor, wherever possible.

FOR PEOPLE LIKE US

This book is for everyday people like us. That is the reason, I give utmost importance to feedback and reviews from everyday people like you and me in choosing how to keep this work updated with latest material, research, and industrial application.

Master everything I am going to teach you here. Then, apply these kick-butt skills at work or business. Work smart and execute ruthlessly. You will be able to make a huge difference. People will find it hard to argue with the real results you will produce. Your impact will be undeniable and people will take notice. Rich rewards await. Let me close with one of my favorite quotes.

> *The greatest danger is not that we aim too high and miss it,*
> *but that we aim too low and reach it.*
> - Michelangelo

If you are holding a copy of this book, my expectation from you is the same as I had in the first book on marketing. I wrote this book for people like us and I cannot wait to see the great things you will do with it.

- Ritesh Chaube

Share your stories at: 200kMBA.com/Leadership/feedback.

xv

CHAPTER ONE

VISIONARY LEADERSHIP

First rule of leadership: everything is your fault.

- From the movie, A Bug's Life

On an early morning of September 1982, twelve-year-old Mary Kellerman of Elk Grove, Illinois, USA takes a capsule of Tylenol and lies down on her bed. She dies within minutes. Later that day, postal employee Adam Janus of Arlington Heights, Illinois dies in the hospital after taking Tylenol. Within the span of next few days seven more people die after taking Tylenol. Doctors determine the cause of death to be poisoning by potassium cyanide. Investigators believe that someone is replacing the bottles of Tylenol at pharmacies and hospitals with those laced with potassium cyanide. This led to an unprecedented public health scare. Johnson & Johnson, owner of Tylenol, has a major crisis on its hands. If you are James Burke, the CEO of Johnson & Johnson at that time, what do you do? More importantly, how do you build a company that can excel in normal business environment while still being able to respond effectively to exceptional situations like crisis? Stay with me. We will cover how visionary leadership can lay the foundation for a great organization.

> *We cannot lead anyone farther than we have been ourselves.*
> -**John C. Maxwell, Author, Speaker, Pastor**

LAYING THE FOUNDATION

If you want to gain followers, become an instagram influencer, not a leader. For the main job of a leader is NOT to lead followers, but to align the resources (people, assets, ideas) of the company with the company's mission while keeping values in mind. You can hire the best employees in the world, but without a clear understanding of your purpose and vision, these employees will be working really hard, but on the wrong thing. There will still be amazing progress, but in the wrong direction. To avoid that leaders must let others see what is inside their minds. They must do that by preparing the Corporate Roadmap. Then, they must tie the Steps on the **Corporate Roadmap** to the various **Management Disciplines** (or practice areas that employees specialize in) to form the **Big Picture** of the company. The idea is that the Big picture helps tie people, assets, task, procedures and everything else inside the company, no matter how big or how small, to the company's mission. Laying out the big picture is a crucial part of laying the foundation of the company.

> *A leader is one who knows the way, shows the way and goes the way.*
> - **John C. Maxwell**

Corporate Roadmap

Leaders must translate the sense of purpose, which exists only their imagination, into a clear path all the way from vision and mission to implementation and control. This is the Corporate Roadmap. Corporate Roadmap must be documented clearly and communicated to the various stakeholders: Board members, management team, employees, partners, vendors, customers, media, local community, and society. An exemplary roadmap for furniture giant IKEA can be found in the Appendix. Here are the steps on a Corporate Roadmap:

- **Purpose**: Raison d'être (French term meaning reason for existence).
- **Values**: Ideals in life that are important to you. Values can include concepts like "equality, honesty, perseverance, loyalty, etc". **Beliefs** are assumptions that we make about the world, based on our past experiences and our mental framework. Values guide you to achieve

your mission using a way that conforms to your Beliefs. You can make a million dollars robbing a bank in a few hours. And take the risks that come with it. Or, you can make a million starting a business that delivers hot meals, which could take a few years. Your values define which route you will take. Values define how you will behave. Values combined with beliefs forms **Culture**.

- **Vision**: Where you want to be in the future.
- **Mission**: What you are going to do now to realize your vision. Now equals Present.
- **Goal**: A specific defined target that needs to be hit to complete the mission. Specify how much (magnitude) and by when (time).
- **Objectives**: Goal broken down into smaller defined milestones. Some times objectives are skipped if the goal is singular and simple.
- **Strategy**: Specific statement of what needs to be done to realize the goals, and hence the mission.
- **Tactics**: Statement of how resources will be allocated and steps that will be followed in coordination to execute the strategy. Tactics answer the following questions: How will it be done? Who will take responsibility for each action? When will they do it by?
- **Implementation**: Executing the Tactics.
- **Control**: measuring the results of implementation and using feedback loop to improve the roadmap from mission to implementation.

Management Disciplines or Practice Areas

Management Disciplines are areas of practice that employees specialize in. Here are the subset of disciplines that Leaders are frequently involved with. (The remaining Management Disciplines are Listed in the Appendix)

Leadership and Organizations involves understanding the principles behind effective leadership and how to use these principles to manage organizations at any scale.

Executive Leadership involves understanding the importance of ethical beliefs, dignity and social values to becoming a globally effective leader.

Crisis Management involves understanding how to deal with disruptive and unexpected events that threatens the organization or its stakeholders.

Strategic Negotiations help understand the negotiation techniques for handling counterparts from different cultural backgrounds at the bargaining table.

Corporate Law helps get a finer understanding of company and contract law and it application to the stages in the life cycle of the corporation.

Corporate Governance involves the mechanisms, relations, and processes by which a corporation is controlled and directed to balance the interests of the stakeholders.

The Big Picture

Finally, the leader must tie the various Management Disciplines that employees specialize in to the Corporate Roadmap to form the Big Pic-

The Big Picture

① PURPOSE & VALUES
- Ethics
- Executive Leadership
- Leadership and Organizations

② VISION
- Ethics
- Leadership and Organizations
- Marketing Management
- Executive Leadership

③ MISSION
- Leadership
- Macroeconomics
- Marketing Management
- Executive Leadership
- Corporate Governance

④ GOAL
- Leadership
- Financial Reporting Systems
- Economics of Competition
- Corporate Law
- Corporate Governance
- Marketing Management
- Marketing Strategy

⑤ STRATEGY
- Marketing Management
- Marketing Strategy
- Strategic Decisions in Operations

⑥-⑦ TACTICS & IMPL.
- Operations Management
- Marketing Management
- Marketing Strategy
- Marketing Tactics
- Mergers & Acquisitions
- Strategic Financial Management
- International Finance
- Managerial Finance
- Managerial Economics
- Statistical Decision Analysis
- Corporate Law

⑧-⑨ CONTROL
- Accounting
- Financial Reporting Systems
- Corporate Law
- Strategic Crisis Management
- Leadership
- Strategic Negotiations
- Operations Management
- Marketing Management
- Marketing Strategy
- Marketing Tactics

ture of the company. The idea is that the Big picture helps tie every task happening inside the company, no matter how big or how small, to the company's mission. I know that am repeating myself here. This is because the idea of Big Picture is of utmost importance. Go over it again if you need to. If you understand that the Corporate Roadmap and the Management Disciplines tie in to form the Big Picture, you understand leadership and management better than 99.5% of the people out there.

The Big Picture maps every thing that should be done to achieve the mission, goals, strategies, etc., to everything that the employees of the company will do. From CEO to the individual employee in operations or accounting, as well as partners, vendors and suppliers. The Big Picture helps individual employees stay connected to the goals of their team and it helps teams stay connected to the mission of the company. It helps everyone in the company know that they are making a clearly defined and positive contribution everyday they come to work.

Look at this another way. If a task an employee is performing cannot be tied back to the mission, that employee's efforts are being wasted. Cut away that task and reassign that employee to perform something task that does tie back, directly or indirectly, to the mission.

WHAT DO LEADERS DO

There are leaders at all levels of an organization from the Board of Directors down to the individual employees. Obviously, we will cover what Boards are and how they work with the CEO and the company in the section on 'Corporate Governance'. If you are a small business owner like a restaurant or a Doctor's Office, all this still applies to you.

It is just that the roles of board of directors and that of the CEO has been rolled up into a single role that is performed by the owner or the whoever owns the small business. You may not have the fancy title, but you still have to perform all the duties that a CEO of a large company does, albeit on a much smaller scale.

> *You may never know what results come of your actions,*
> *but if you do nothing, there will be no results.*
> *- Mahatma Gandhi*

Leadership inside the Boards

Board of Directors are usually successful high-power individuals appointed by the shareholders/owners that govern the company from the outside. Board members play a very significant role in providing guidance to company by contributing to the organization's culture, strategic focus, effectiveness, and financial sustainability, as well as serving as ambassadors and advocates. The members of the Board are not employees of the company. The CEO, who is the employee of the company, has a seat at the Board. Formally, the CEO is the board's connection to the company, though sometimes the Board members will be in touch with Senior management (including President or the COO who reports to the CEO) to get a feel for how things are going. The Board is led by the Chairman. In some cases, the Chairman and the CEO are one (and it does lead to one powerful individual who can cause of lot of good or a lot of damage depending on which side of the bed he wakes up on any given day. Think of Elon Musk at Tesla).

When you can't make them see the light, make them feel the heat.
- Ronald Reagan

As a Leader, Chairman should align the incentives of the CEO with mission of the organization. Chairman should ensure that the CEO and the senior executives bear the risk of ownership of the company just as the shareholders do. Chairman should also make sure that the CEO and the senior executives are rewarded for delivering superior long term returns rather than short term quarter over quarter magic.

Stanislav Shekshnia, Professor at the INSEAD business school hit the nail on the head when it comes to qualities that are essential for a Chairman. Since, boards are composed of senior, successful, action-oriented, performance-driven, sophisticated individuals from different backgrounds and countries, managing these relations requires exceptional behavioral or soft skills. In addition, as a Leader, the Chairman must imbibe humility, ego suppression, energetic presence, passion, patience and self-reflection.

Chairman should engage the board members to be physically present, be emotionally involved, and work effectively as a group by actively leaving their outside interests outside. Chairman should also make sure that the board's agenda contains strategic, ripe-for-discussion items nobody else inside the company can handle. Chairman should focus on enabling others to speak their mind and encourage the board as a whole to make decisions rather than dominating the group process.

Leadership at CEO Level

Leadership is about gaining alignment with the mission and values of the organization.

-Bill George, Former CEO, Medtronic

The primary role of a CEO is to help the company gaining alignment with its mission and values. Accordingly, a CEO must spearhead the development of the **Corporate Roadmap** (if one doesn't exist or does not have enough clarity) and tie the **Management Disciplines or Practice Areas** inside the company to from the **Big Picture** of managing the company. Obviously since completing the Big Picture requires working at various levels of details, the senior managers and mid-level managers should be involved. The CEO must define the Vision and the Mission of the company while keeping the Purpose and Values in mind.

Another important role of a CEO is to make sure that value proposition and incentives of the various stake holders (board, employees, management team, vendors, customers, media, local community, society) are aligned. This simply means that the stakeholders must have something to lose if they don't act in way that is beneficial to the mission of the organization. Here are some examples of incentives that each stake holders could have to keep them aligned.

- Board: Performance based vested stock ownership
- Employees: Continued employment, competitive benefits, Performance based vested stock ownership.

- Management team: Continued employment, Performance based vested stock ownership.
- Vendors: Continued business and contracts renewals.
- Customers: Innovative value-added products and services, continued support on products.
- Media: Paid press releases, access to product launches and breaking news, social responsibility.
- Local community: Local employment, economic development.
- Society: Growth, Innovation.

Value proposition and incentives keep the stake holders in check and make job of running the company a lot easier. CEO should align the incentives of the Senior and Mid-Level executives with the goals and strategies of the organization by rewarding them for delivering superior multiyear value.

Harry Kraemer, ex-CEO of Baxter and my professor, is my favorite when it comes to describing qualities essential to a CEO. In his book, "From Values to Action," exhorts leaders to always do the right thing. He cites four principles that are important to values based leadership: Self reflection, Balance, True self confidence, and Genuine humility. The importance of Value system to CEO leadership cannot be overemphasized. As a leader, you will have your fair share of difficult decisions. And, in times of difficult decisions, values will guide you. He advocates inspiration by setting examples rather than verbal motivation. Harry encourages leaders to empower the team by giving responsibility, establishing accountability and setting the team up for success. He wants leaders to maintain a global perspective and exhibit social responsibility by deal with changes, controversy, and crisis with courage and swiftness. Finally, Harry maintains that as leaders, CEOs must adjust to cultural differences. This is especially important for CEOs that run global companies. Genuine humility and respect for culture is an essential quality here. He advises that it would be smart to have a trusted man in each global region and to take time to get tips from this trusted man to get to know the regional culture.

Leadership in Senior Management

The primary role of leadership at senior management is to align the activities of the different departments with the Goals and Strategies of the company.

> *Strategic leaders must not get consumed by the operational and tactical side of their work. They have a duty to find time to shape the future.*
>
> - **Stephanie S. Mead, Senior Vice President of CMOE**

Senior managers, including the President, must assist the CEO in preparing the Big Picture of Management of the company by taking the lead in goal planning and strategic planning. Their active involvement is important here because the CEO is not going to know details of business practice and the issues involved therein that seem obvious to people who work on and deal with them everyday.

> *It is necessary for us to learn from others' mistakes. You will not live long enough to make them all yourself.*
>
> - **Admiral Hyman G. Rickover**

It is valuable for the CEO to learn and benefit from the mistakes the Senior Managers have made and to give them the respect and platform to voice their input and ideas. Senior managers must align the incentives of the middle managers and front-line employees with the organization's strategic plan and tactical plan by rewarding them for delivering on Key Performance Areas.

Leadership in Middle Management

The primary role of leadership at middle management is to align the priority and allocation of resources of the individual departments with the Tactical plan of the company as well as develop detailed plans for execution, measurement and control.

Mid-level managers must assist the Senior managers and the CEO in preparing the Big Picture of Management of the company by taking the lead in Tactical planning. Again, active involvement is crucial here because the senior managers are not going to know details of individual departments and the issues involved therein that seem obvious to people who work on everyday. Senior Management must completely refrain from micromanagement and trust and empower the mid-level managers to lead the development of tactical plans for their departments.

The key to being a good manager is keeping the people who hate you away from those who are still undecided.

- Some smart ass

At the middle and lower level of the company, it is a lot of dog-eat-dog world. Layoffs, competitions for promotions, salary increments, and better perks leads to unhealthy intra-team competition. Accordingly, the primary goal of communication at these levels should be to put their mind at ease and instill in them a sense of security about their place in the company. Leaders must convince these ranks that the organization appreciates what they have done thus far. Moreover, they value team members more for what they bring to the table and what they can do for the organization in the future. Make employees feel secure in their jobs. Make them feel that helping the team is good for their personal career growth. Leader should clarify that the company values team contributions as much as individual contributions in deciding employee. That way, employees will not be worried that if they delegate or teach everything they know about an intricate business process to someone new, their jobs will be at risk. If they delegate, they will then grow in their roles and move up the hierarchy. Not because they are taking over someone else role and that person is getting fired. But, because the company is growing and there are more people and assets to manage and so everyone grows with the company. When this is explicitly said, it will make sense to the team. They will find it logical and won't dismiss this as leadership drivel. They will internalize it and practice it everyday. And, that will create a strong culture of helpful work ethic in the company.

LEADERS MUST DEFINE THE VISION

I think that the greatest gift humans have is not the gift of sight but the gift of vision. Sight is a function of the eyes, but vision is a function of the heart & mind.

- Myles Munroe

Vision statement is a concise description of where you want to be in the future. It is a statement of corporate dreams. For without dreams, better future wouldn't be possible. Vision must derive from purpose and values. Vision guides Mission and everything else that comes after it. From Goals and Strategy, all the way to control. Your purpose, and therefore your vision, should be an extension of you. You must believe in it. Without that true belief, you will not have the perseverance to follow through with it. Steve Jobs said that.

Without a clear understanding of your Vision, you will be lost about your place and position in the market. Basically, you will have no strategy, and therefore, no business. If you are starting a new line of business, your vision should align not only with your purpose and values, but also with your core competencies. You should already have these competencies or have the resources to develop them.

Writing a vision statement

So, how do you write a vision statement? A Vision statement can be a single line or several paragraphs in length. Your time horizon should be five plus years. It should be written in simple language and business speak should be avoided as much as possible. A Vision statement should encompass your aspirations and should be inspiring to stakeholders. Vision statement should be updated once the vision is realized or if a careful analysis of competitive and regulatory factors indicates that realizing the mission would be impossible.

LEADERS MUST DEFINE THE MISSION

Vision without action is merely a dream. Action without vision just passes the time. Vision with action can change the world.

- Joel Blake

Mission statement describes clearly what you are going to do now to realize your Vision. When you know what your mission is, you can start working towards it, rather than sitting on the sidelines and worrying about it or judging others in the arena. Mission statement should state what the company will do now, how it will do it and why it does it. The why part comes from vision and purpose. Mission statement should, also define, as briefly as possible, what the organization is doing for customers, employees, owners, collaborators, and community. If you are a large enterprise, the world will be your community because your impact will likely be global.

Writing a mission statement

So, how do you write a mission statement? Mission statement should be no longer than a short paragraph. Better if it is just a sentence or two. This makes it easier to showcase and make it easy for the audience to remember. Some experts are of the opinion that mission statement should be written by involving everyone. But, I disagree. We have tried it multiple times and it just leads to a ginormous waste to time. The clarity of thinking needed to compose something as important as a mission statement is uncommon. It can come only after intensive training, years of top management experience or if you take the time to read high quality material. Let us drink our own kool-aid here and state that you will be ready because you are reading this book. Mostly, you will be better than most out there once you are done with this book. Once the mission statement is ready, however, it should be reviewed by everyone. They can offer their inputs. Why? Because now there is a solid core upon which the statement can be refined. The team should read the mission statement. And, then you should wait if someone needs an explanation. If they do, then you need to reword and revise. Because, the end goal is that the mission should resonate with everyone without requiring a clarification. This may take countless revisions. But it is important that one understands it the first time they read it. Another useful idea is to give an employee or a vendor a blind screening test by asking them to read your mission statement among three or four other mission statements. They should be able to identify which one is yours. If not, you need to revise and reword and rework. This process can be frustrating but it is completely worth it. The best mission statement will become the company slogan. As your company evolves, the mission statement should be revised. That is because no company ever stays exactly the same.

LEADERS MUST ESTABLISH VALUES & CULTURE

Failure leaves no ambiguity. It is absolute. Most failures in business are failure of leadership stemming from lack of ethics, which in turn stem from lack of a strong system of values and culture. That is why leaders have the ultimate responsibility when it comes to grooming ethical standards in the enterprise. Sometimes, this might entail making the hard choices. You may have to let go of the finest craftsmen in the industry or that genius technologist, if their immoral conduct does not conform to the ethical framework of the company, inspire of repeated training and corrections. When it comes to people, as a leader, the primary task is to get the wrong people off the bus, get the right people on the bus, and put the right people in the right seats.

Leader must clearly state the values and the culture and then create a strong following of this culture. This will influence the team to assimilate the statement of values and conduct themselves ethically. If a slippage do occur, and they will, employees will be more likely to report the wrongdoing to management because employees feel safe and confident that the issue they are reporting will be handled fairly.

Moreover, teams who have ethical leaders report more favorable job attitudes such as job satisfaction and commitment. This is because followers are attracted to ethical role models who care about them, treat them fairly, and set high ethical standards.

Management is doing things right; leadership is doing the right things

- Peter Drucker

A strong system of ethics shows it true worth in times of crises. It leaves little doubt for what should be done. It simply says, "Do the right thing". Back to the Tylenol crises. What do you do if you are James Burke, CEO of J&J in 1982 and you are faced with cyanide-laced Tylenol in Chicago drugstores and seven people are dead? J&J quickly established that the cyanide lacing occurred after cases of Tylenol left the factory. In J&J's defense, Police issued a statement that someone must have taken bottles off the shelves of local grocers and drug stores in the Chicago area, laced the capsules with poison, and then returned the restored packages to the shelves to be purchased by the unknowing victims. But, Burke did not stop there. Burke did the right thing even though it was a huge financial hit for J&J. Burke and J&J took an active role with the media in issuing mass warning communications. Burke ordered immediate recall of 31 million bottles and set up a crisis hotline to answer consumers' questions. J&J offered replacement capsules to those who turned in pills already purchased and a reward for anyone with information leading to the apprehension of those involved in these murders.

Burke reiterated that the company's values, which put customers before corporate profits, helped to guide decision making throughout the firm during the crisis. Experts believed that this crisis would bankrupt the company. But, Burke went onto develop the tamper resistant packaging. Restored consumer faith in the company through his ethical leadership and successfully rebuilt the brand.

RECAP

In this chapter, we looked at what it takes to be a Visionary Leader. Not just a leader, but the one who leads with Vision. We accomplished this by first understanding that sometimes Leaders can be lonely visionaries who must then lay the foundation of the organization and form the Big picture of the company to let others see what is inside their minds. Next, we looked at what leaders should do inside the board of directors, CEO level and the senior and middle management levels. This was followed by a subsection on how leaders should define the vision and the mission. Finally, we look at how leaders should establish Value and culture within the organization. In the next few sections, we will look at everything else leaders must do.

ACTION ITEM

Checkout the blank template of the Roadmap in the Appendix. Make a copy of the Roadmap and use it to think through how you would create the Roadmap for your personal life, the business you own, or the company you work for.

VISIONARY LEADERSHIP 21

CHAPTER TWO

LEADERSHIP IN ACTION

One of the things I've always found is that you've got to start with the customer experience and work backwards to the technology. You can't start with the technology and try to figure out where you're going to try to sell it. And I've made this mistake probably more than anybody else in this room. And, I got the scar tissue to prove it.

- **Steve Jobs on leading transformational change**

I admire Late Steve Jobs for reasons other than the rest of the world does. For something he didn't have to do. Steve was a very, very rich before iPod and iPhone. He could have easily led his life being nice to people, just living famously in silicon valley, making safe bets along the way, and he still would have made out like a bandit.

But, Steve chose the difficult path of reinventing the music industry and the smartphone. That is very hard to do. Why? Being an engineer, I will tell you one thing. Most engineers will push back on everything that is not possible with the current technology. And, that is what has resulted historically in ordinary phones like Motorola Razrs, Palm Pilots and Blackberry Storms. They let you do what you need to do, but there is nothing seductive about them. To reinvent the smartphone, the envelope has to be pushed way past what is possible.

Steve had to say fuck you to a lot of engineers who said, "No, that is not possible" and ask them to go back to their drawing boards to come up with a way to do what he wanted done. That might have been the reason he got progressively angrier and angrier with the passing years and got labelled the "mega asshole". Try working in a company where 90% of the employees despise you for pushing them so hard and causing years and years of time away from kids, missed piano recitals, working over weekends, and passively angry spouses.

Prior to the iPhone, plastic screens were standard on smartphones. About six months before the iPhone was released in 2007, Jobs became worried after using the prototype iPhone that the device's display would get scratched when the phone jumbled around in pant or purse pockets with keys and coins. Jobs called Corning's CEO, Wendell Weeks, and asked him if Corning could create a glass cover that would resist scratches and breakage. Corning usually requires two years of R&D before rolling a new product out, but, Steve persuaded Corning to get it done in six months — an almost impossible feat. The result was Gorilla Glass, which defined the feel of the user's finger moving around on the touchscreen. It is the superior tactile experience, combined with the responsive graphic software, that was iPhone's seductive magic. Most major smartphone manufacturers followed suit and started using some version of Gorilla glass to replicate the similar feel of touch. My point is: **Leaders should be agents of change and improvement.** This takes a lot of daring and initiative.

Much of the advice on leadership is very pedantic. As if a saint is preaching it: "You should be this. You should be that. Do only this. Don't do that". That simply makes reading anything on this topic so boring. Let's change that. Let's do that by using lively examples, honest analysis and straying closer to controversy by looking at the dark side of leadership. In this section, we will cover the importance of principles of ethics to becoming a globally effective leader and using these principles behind effective leadership to manage organizations at any scale.

Let me ask you a question. What is the difference between a boss and a leader? Two words: Courage & Humility. A True leader has humility while the boss does not. Humility is the reason that there are many bosses, but very few leaders.

Jesus exemplified the kind of compassionate and humble leadership he wanted from his disciples by washing their feet. This was the task of the lowest ranked servants at that time. Later, Prophet Mohammed and Mahatma Gandhi followed that inspiration by kindling the similar humble style of leadership in their followers.

> *A true leader has the confidence to stand alone, the courage to make tough decisions, and the compassion to listen to the needs of others.*
> - General Douglas MacArthur

Courage gives leaders the strength to make the right decisions, no matter how painful, and take responsibility for the outcome. But, humility empowers leaders to realize that they need others and to listen to them. Humility also allows leaders to acknowledge mistakes and change course if a decision turns out to be wrong, and share the success with others when things work out.

DARK SIDE OF LEADERSHIP

Compromise around ethics is responsible for a lion's share of interesting news headlines around the world, including shady schemes, cheating, scandals, price-fixing, insider trading, bribery, harassment, sexual misconduct, faulty products, etc. Notable examples include the Enron scandal in 2001, which cost shareholders $74 billion; the Freddie Mac scandal in 2003, in which the federally backed mortgage financing company was caught lying about $5 billion in earnings; and the largest Ponzi scheme spun by Bernie Madoff in which he tricked investors out of $64.8 billion.

When unethical business practices become public knowledge, it usually results in falling stock prices, recalls and fixes, investigations, lawsuits. The company loses reputation, credibility, brand following, and what usually follows is the possible liquidation of the corporation itself, and extinction of the brand.

> *There are three kinds of men. The one that learns by reading. The few who learn by observation. The rest of them have to pee on the electric fence for themselves.*
>
> *- Will Rogers*

Leaders must realize that they are watched and scrutinized all the time. They will always be in the spotlight. Accordingly, it is easier to lead with ethics and commonsense in the long term. Ethics establish a moral compass of right and wrong and often when the law fails, it is the ethics that saves the leader from acting against the greater good.

Traits that drive leadership in wrong direction

It doesn't help that the human mind, in all its virtues, is a warehouse of psychological cognitive biases (in case you were curious, psychology is the study of conscious and unconscious behavior and mind, whereas cognitive science is the study of mind and its processes. And I promise I will explain what biases are). In the mind-blowing book "Thinking Fast and Slow," Nobel prize winning psychologist Daniel Kahneman describes how internal biases shape our beliefs and encourage our own minds to mislead us. We make hundreds or even thousands of decisions every day. What should I eat for lunch? Which shoes should I wear today? Should I drive or take the bus? Our minds are constantly looking to conserve energy. So we develop mental shortcuts to more easily process new information and make difficult decisions. Psychologists have a name for these mental shortcuts: Heuristics. A heuristic is an approach to problem solving developed by our brain. Heuristics help our brains substitute simpler but related questions with more complex and difficult questions. Heuristics are fast and usually correct. But, they don't always work perfectly. So our brains have a tendency to use them to form beliefs. Why do our brains from beliefs? Because our brains are lazy. Smart albeit lazy sloths. Our brains, go one step further and try to combine heuristics (which are already shortcuts) into shortcuts. This greed to form beliefs leads to prejudices, which are simply incorrect beliefs. Psychologists have a name for these prejudices: Biases. Heuristics, unavoidably, impact our decision making and lead to biases. Bias cause smart well-intentioned leaders to make poor decisions.

Leadership Heuristics & Biases

Decisions	Heuristics	Beliefs
Which shoes should I wear?	Black heels look great on all outfits	Black heels look great on all outfits
Is this lipstick color good?	Red color goes with all my dresses	Right combo of colors is important for a balanced fashion sense
Slice of pizza or Green Soup	Green soup is healthier than pizza	Eating healthier is important for good health

Whether we realize it or not, we are all biased. If we are aware of these biases, we can do our best to save ourselves from falling victim to them. So, the takeaway is: heuristics help make life easier and allow us to make quicker decisions that are usually pretty accurate. But, these heuristics can lead to potential biases and being mindful of them will help us make better and more accurate decisions.

The best we can do is a compromise: learn to recognize situations in which mistakes are likely and try harder to avoid significant mistakes when the stakes are high.

- Daniel Kahneman

Here are some biases that compromise our capabilities as effective leaders.

Halo Effect

In an interesting study, Polish American Psychologist Solomon Asch described two people, Alan and Ben, and asked participants what they thought of their personalities.

Alan: intelligent, industrious, impulsive, critical, stubborn, envious

Ben: envious, stubborn, critical, impulsive, industrious, intelligent

If you're like most people, you saw Alan much more positively than Ben. Why? Read again, the exact same traits are listed for each person. Just in a different order. Positive traits appear for Alan earlier in the list. Negative traits appear earlier in the list for Ben. Kahneman referred to this study and later explained that the initial traits in the list change the very meaning of the traits that appear later. The stubbornness of an intelligent person is seen as likely to be justified and may actually evoke respect, but intelligence in an envious and stubborn person makes him more dangerous.

> *What the human being is best at doing is interpreting all new information so that their prior conclusions remain intact.*
>
> - Warren Buffett

Confirmation bias

This bias relates to the human tendency to seek information that supports our existing beliefs. Conspiracy theories are prime examples of the confirmation bias. If you're convinced man didn't really set foot on the moon, you'll find plenty of evidence to support that belief, and you'll ignore evidence that disproves it. Absence of evidence is not evidence of absence.

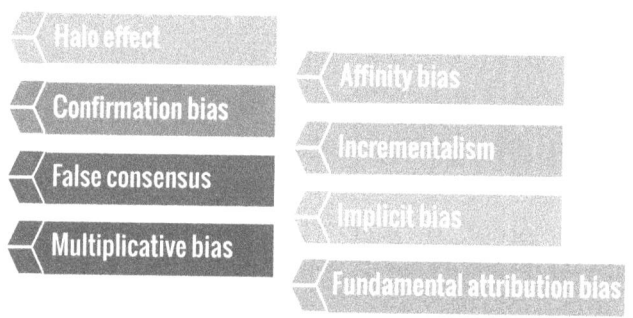

Major Leadership Biases

In the 1960s, cognitive psychologist Peter Cathcart Wason conducted a number of experiments known as Wason's rule discovery task. Participants were given the sequence of number e.g. "2-4-6". Then, they were asked to formulate a simple hypothesis about the rule. Most people felt that this was a sequence of even numbers. Then they were asked to test this rule by proposing more sequences of numbers that follow this rule. Participants proposed: "4-8-10," "6-8-12," "20-22-24". In response to this, the participants were told that these sequences did follow the rule. Most participants felt confident about the "sequence of even numbers" hypothesis. The only thing is, this wasn't the rule. The rule was much simpler. Simply increasing numbers. Most participants tried number sequences that only prove their hypothesis and very few actually tried to make up a number sequence that might disprove their hypothesis. The participants did not ask questions to falsify their hypothesis because as much as possible, they do not want to break their own rules.

Quine and Ullian wrote, in their book called Web of belief, something that I found very profound: The desire to be right and the desire to have been right are two desires, and the sooner we separate them the better off we are. The desire to be right is the thirst for truth. On all counts, both practical and theoretical, there is nothing but good to be said for it. The desire to have been right, on the other hand, is the pride that goeth before a fall. It stands in the way of our seeing we were wrong, and thus blocks the progress of our knowledge.

To become capable leaders, we must actively seek evidence that challenges our initial impressions. We need to ask not just "Could I be wrong?", but also, "How am I wrong?".

Multiplicative bias

What is 1025 x 356 x 78 x 60 x 0?

You are sharp. It is zero. Notice the 0 at the end. Anything multiplied by 0 is 0. In most cars, if a tire blows out, the engine won't be of much use. If the engine breaks down, the leather wrapped steering wheel will amount to nothing. Each of these components offers a potential zero that can throw off the entire system. A car is an example of a multiplicative system as opposed to an additive system. How is this all relevant? We like to think of things as additive rather than multiplicative. Because, it makes it easier to deal with them. It is easier to go buy a bottle of glue from the store than to search the house to find where you keep it the last time you used it. It is easier and exciting to ask people to go build something new than to do the trial and errors to painstakingly locate the fault within the current system.

Businesses operate as multiplicative systems. But, most people wrongly assume that business are more like additive systems. Many CEO's will prioritize resources to add more features to their products, instead of providing helpful documentation or support (a primary reason that customers could be leaving, never to return). They think that tacking a 1025 on 356 x 78 x 60 x 0 will help. But, that 0 is what needs to be taken care of instead of piling on more features. Your 0 could be anything. You just have to realize that there could be a zero and that finding and fixing this zero can significant headway towards the goal.

Multiplicative bias is even more powerful when it comes to people. All the work ethic and intelligence in the world won't matter if someone lacks integrity. And no amount of talent and skills will account for someone who rubs people the wrong way and makes enemies with every interaction.

Fundamental attribution bias

This bias makes people over emphasize personal characteristics and ignore situational factors when judging the behavior of others. As an example, if an employee frequently shows up late for work, we might think that they are lazy and unmotivated. But, what if you found out that they have a demanding responsibility at home to care for a sick family? In this case, allowing them to work from home or staggering their work hours could help the employee be productive while coping with the situation. The takeaway is that we must try to understand what other possible explanations there might be for the undesirable behavior we are seeing.

Here are some other biases that affect most leaders:

False consensus is a bias that causes people to overestimate the likelihood that others think and act in the same way that they do.

Implicit biases causes people to have attitudes towards others or associate stereotypes with them without conscious knowledge.

Incrementalism causes leaders to slide unintentionally into unethical behavior over time in small steps.

Affinity bias relates to the predisposition we all have to favor people who remind us of ourselves.

These biases cause leaders to fall prey to or commit the many errors of judgement some of which are listed below:

Planning fallacy causes leaders to underestimate the amount of time and resources it takes to accomplish a task.

Lack of trust in the ability of others causes leaders to micromanage.

People pleaser tendency causes leaders to be overly focused on wanting to be liked.

Excessively directive tendency causes leaders to adopt a style where they are 'telling' rather than showing your team what needs to be done. This goes against the golden rule of: Don't demand action, don't command action, inspire action.

Inability to shield the team from external pressures and pressure from the hierarchy. Examples of such pressures are bureaucratic pressures, time constraints, and lack of information or resources.

Missing changes happening in the competitive landscape. This is likely due to confirmation bias, where we erroneously filter out anything that does not fit our preconceived notions or beliefs.

Vices that drive leadership in wrong direction

What else steers leaders in the wrong direction? How about the vices: alcohol, gambling, adulteration, and of course the master of them all, Mr. Money? Money is colossal cause of ethical compromise in leadership. Mainly, because it lets you buy most of the other vices. The rest is mostly sex, professional jealousy or rivalry. I would never advise you to stay away from vices. Because, life is just not fun without these vices. I would only advise that it needs to be in moderation. You must always be aware that these vices are like fire. Like a candle flame that can consume the very house it provides light to.

Don't get into lifestyle that will demand more money than you can afford to spend. Remember. If you are compromised, you lose you reputation. And, if you lose reputation, you lose everything. That is the reason leaders must observe a fair degree of personal discipline. Don't get attached to money. Even, if you are making tons of it. Which is likely because successful leaders do get paid way more than average. As you climb the corporate ladder, control how much you let wealth influence your living. Otherwise, eventually, you will upgrade your life style and start hanging out with those who have way more money. Suddenly, you might find yourself in a lifestyle where you are spending more than you are making, just to keep up with them. And, this will sow the seeds of compromise in your ethics and your leadership. Don't go there. Don't put yourself in a position where you have to do something unethical to save face. Besides, affluent spending may impress them in the short run. But, in the long run, people like and form lifelong bonds with good people who can be trusted and have morals.

Social factors that drive leadership in the wrong direction

If the mental biases and the easily available vices like gambling, adultery and addiction were not enough, we have social factors that can drive leadership in the wrong direction.

For the longest time, experts and gurus preached the old science of leadership which stated that technical skills are an indispensable part of leadership. They preached that capable leaders must possess all the skills to perform the job of any other member on the team. If leaders don't have these skills, they must acquire it through training. I think the old science of leadership was fascinated and seduced by intellectual genius. The sort of genius that Actor Matt Damon's character possessed in the movie Good Will Hunting where he was brilliant at mathematics, literature and history. In most workplaces, who would possess all the skills needed to perform all the tasks in a department? Somebody who has spent 30 years of their career there. Would that make them a good leader? Certainly not. They deserve seniority, respect and proportional pay, but will they have the chops to be a good leader? Moreover, does one really have to spend 30 years climbing the ranks in technical positions to become a leader. I don't think that should be a necessity. Frequently, leaders that did not have the technical skills and had too much ego to admit that they "don't know how to fix it" would start faking or taking credit for other people's work. If they did not have the humility to spend time with a specialist to learn the skills, they would just say that they fix it instead of giving credit to the specialist who actually fixed it and deserves the credit.

The new science of leadership takes a more logical approach. It decouples skills from leadership. It says: Adapt whatever skills you have to the situation at hand and access skills you don't have, but need right now, through others, especially if you cannot learn and get good at it quickly. And, give credit to other who help you out. Saying, "I don't know," "I need help," "Thank you for helping me" are powerful ways to access the skills of the tribe and form a bond. Consulting companies like Mckinsey and Accenture do this all the time. For each client project, teams are chosen by senior project managers from their pool of global talent based and assembled based on the needs of the particular project. In such teams, the most effective leaders are facilitators/orchestrators, not skilled technicians. The new science of leadership also says that having different leaders for different situations is not entirely a bad idea. This is where it takes an understanding leader to keep his ego aside and allow someone else, as well as themselves, to be led by another individual who possesses better leadership experience in the specific situation at hand.

SUCCEEDING AS A LEADER IN TEAMS

> *It is a terrible thing to look over your shoulder when you are trying to lead — and find no one there.*
>
> \- Franklin Roosevelt

Every organization has a formal structure and an informal structure/network. The same is true of teams. Formal structure in this context indicates the hierarchical reporting structure. Informal structure indicates people or groups (called 'cliques') that connect with each other on a personal level. They usually go out together for lunch or happy hours after work, or their kids play baseball together on the weekend. The formal structure is easily visible. However, you must understand the informal structure of the organization to win. How people form connection with others or how people organize into informal groups is governed by some well laid out principle of networking:

- Self similarity principle: We find comfort in connecting with people who are similar to us because it inspires innate trust, comfort zone, utility, self affirmation and joy of agreement.
- Shared activity principle: Team sports, boards, community service, cross functional teams, volunteer groups are examples of shared activities which inspire passion, interdependence and a sense of connection between participants even if the participants are from vastly different backgrounds.
- Proximity principle: Frequent interactions increase the number of times individuals are in close proximity and this helps form bonds

and connections. Lawyers of opposing parties are known to form a bond, over a course of time, as they see the other lawyers multiple times during arbitration or trials. They are known to go out for lunch together before heading into a court ordered mediation where they pretend to have heated arguments for their clients.

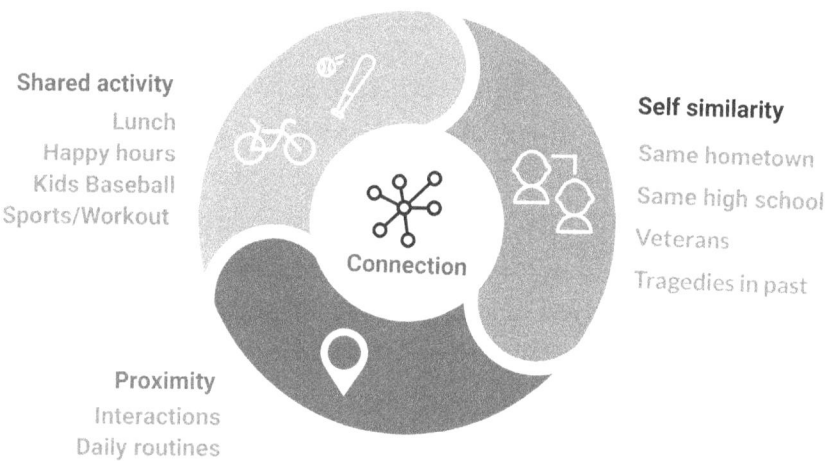

Formation of Social Connections

Shared activity
Lunch
Happy hours
Kids Baseball
Sports/Workout

Self similarity
Same hometown
Same high school
Veterans
Tragedies in past

Connection

Proximity
Interactions
Daily routines

If you have been brought in to implement a change, let me say that you don not have an easy way ahead of you. Implementing change in teams you have a rapport with is hard enough. Implementing change within teams that you have just joined is twice as hard. People don't like change. And, they certainly don't like change coming from someone new. Every change you impose will use up your social and political capital. In the classic movie, Prestige, Nikola Tesla is attempting to convince Magician Angier (played by Sir Hugh Jackman... I am 'hugh' fan of him) that he should not make too many changes in his magic act. Tesla says. "The first time I brought about change, people hailed me as a visionary. The second time, they politely asked me to leave".

Whether you are bringing about change or are simply installed in a team to supercharge the key performance numbers, you will face opposition. Here are some rules for dealing with people at your level from whom you sense adversarial pushback.

- Use Redirection: If you sense a lot of opposition or pushback from someone who has a lot of informal influence within the team, you can start a dialog with them, by saying, for example, "Look, I didn't put us in this situation."
- Use Reciprocity: Give before asking. Use words like, "We can help each other."
- Use Rationality: "I can do a lot of good for both of us. So, help me or stay outta my way."

With people who are above you in the formal hierarchy, you will have to be a lot more diplomatic and humble. Keep in mind that people in power will not give you the time of the day without reason. They need a reason to interact with someone lower in the hierarchy. And, people in power mostly don't need you. You need them:

- Use Redirection: Serve them. Trying saying, "I am just a catalyst and I am here to assist you."
- Reciprocity: "I can help improve your bottom line."
- Rationality: "I have the corporate resources to help you achieve your goals."

Use of redirection, reciprocity and rationality is important in situations where you are walking in with low trust. Your success hinges upon how quickly you can build relationships. And, to build relationship under distrust, the emotional state must be addressed by using redirection and reciprocity, otherwise, all the efforts, data, facts, evidence (rationality) will be wasted because the person will be incapable of seeing your point of view because they inherently don't want you to win their approval.

ACTIONS IN LEADERSHIP

- Build Teams
- Empower
- Delegate
- Communicate
- Give responsibility
- Establish accountability
- Never micromanage
- Make decisions
- Persuade
- Convince
- Influence
- Inspire
- Negotiate
- Deal with change
- Deal with conflicts
- Deal with crisis

What should leaders embody

Simply put, leaders should develop the people they work with, develop the organization, develop the community & society, and finally develop themselves. To borrow from the golden rule of Boy Scouts, Leaders must "Leave the camp ground cleaner than they found it." In his widely regarded book, 'Good to great,' Jim Collins, maintains that individuals range from level 1 to 5 depending on their ability to lead. Level 1 describes an individual contributor who makes a great employee, but not much of a team player. Level 2 describes a team player who can productively work with other people in a group. Level 3 describes a manager who has the ability to organize a group effectively to achieve specific goals and objectives. Level 4 describes a leader who can power a department or organization to meet performance objectives and achieve a vision. This is the category that most top leaders fall into. Level 5 de-

Principles of Level 5 leadership - Jim Collins

True Leader

OK Leader

Manager

Team Player

Employee

scribes the true leader who embodies the perfect blend of personal humility and professional will.

Personal Humility:

- Deflects attention
- Stands over charisma and leads with inspiring standard
- Grooms a successor
- Gives credit to others

Professional will

- A performance catalyst
- Does whatever it takes
- Builds for the long term
- Takes blame for poor results

A practical way of understanding the principles of Level 5 leadership would be to take a well known leader and see how he stack up against them. Let's pick Richard Branson. What is more fun than judging a billionaire! Sir Richard Charles Nicholas Branson is a self-made billionaire and the flamboyant founder of Virgin Group, which, according to Wikipedia, comprises of more than 400 companies including Virgin Blue airlines, Virgin Galactic Space travel, Virgin mobile and many others. I have never met Richard in person, but I hear from those who have that he is a "Rockstar, without the band, with the entourage, without the attitude". His book 'Business Stripped bare,' which, by the way, is a fantastic read, describes him as an iconic entrepreneur and a "Tie-loathing adventurer and thrill seeker, who believes in turning ideas into reality. Otherwise known as Dr Yes at @virgin!"

Richard Branson - Level 5 leadership

So how will we do it? We will grade Richard on each of the eight traits of Level 5 leaders on a scale from 1 (representing poor) to 10 representing (excellent). If Richard scores more than 90%, he is a level 5 leader. To correctly judge his score, we will search the popular media to locate instances where his behavior and actions aligned with the given trait or performed negatively on the given trait.

Personal Humility

Deflects attention

We will understandably have an uphill task justifying that Richard deflects attention considering the colorful personality that he is well known for. Richard is a celebrity by choice and he plays the part very well. He actively advocates that a leader should take every opportunity, and even drop everything, should a chance to talk to reporters or an interview with media comes up. In fact, celebrity talent international has him available for appearances in advertisements as well as endorsements with prices ranging from $150k to $500k. His flamboyance ranges from appearing dressed up as an air-hostess with red lip color on to an Indian musician while doing a promotional event in Mumbai to appearing wearing only a cellphone in 2002 while promoting Virgin Mobile.

However, Richard's overtures cannot be simply dismissed as a craving for media attention. We must consider that Virgin companies usually broach their way into new markets as "underdogs" with relatively slim marketing budgets. It helps if the CEO is ready to put his ego aside and get down to business to help promote the company in compelling ways which not only capture the attention of the media, but also provide a socially viral way for getting the word out about the product or service.

Richard's score : 5 out of 10

Stands over charisma and Leads with inspiring standard

Richard has had his share of failures ranging from Virgin Vodka to Virgin Brides (wedding dress business) to the cosmetics business Virgin Vie among many others like Virgin cars, Virginware (lingerie). As BusinessInsider reports, when Virgin Vie failed, Virgin paid £8.8 million in 'Brand Protection' money to new management and wrote off £21million in loans as it made its way out the door.

Richard once said: "Business opportunities are like buses, there's always another one coming". He did not let his professional ego keep him in the business. In each of his failures, Richard adopted the corporate standard of admitting failures with determination, cutting down his losses before they balloon and devour the parent enterprise. He took the failures in his stride and then gracefully moved on to lead his troops into the next venture.

Richard's score: 9 out of 10

Grooms a successor

Richard, when asked for advice for new CEOs, said in a television interview: "Find your successor and teach that person everything you know. That way you can focus on the bigger things."

The interviewer asked: "But, wouldn't finding and developing your successor be intimidating for some leaders"

Richard Said: "They are weak leaders"

In each line of business, Richard has a fully capable team of executives who can run the show without Richard's presence. He gives them full autonomy to make business decision, although they check back with him for his business acumen. Virgin Blue had Brett Godfrey. Moreover, Richard has an Investment Advisory team consisting of Gordon McAllum, whom he whisked away from Mckinsey, among others. This team knows everything about the Virgin Global business and can take over in his absence.

Richard's score: 9 out of 10

Gives credit to others

While Richard keeps the media lime-lights for himself, he is not too shy about giving credit where it is due. In his book 'Business Stripped Bare,' he gives plenty of credit to Brett Godfrey for the success of Virgin Blue. His credit wasn't just in verbal terms. He made sure that if Virgin

Blue succeeded, Brett would be compensated in monetary terms for his efforts. Brett made A$80m along the way and is among the richest Australians, due to Virgin Blue. In his book, 'Losing my Virginity,' Richard gives plenty of credit to his team acknowledging that Virgin's success could not have happened without them. As noted on kissmetrics.com, Richard once said: "A company is simply a group of people. And as a leader of people, you have to be a great listener, you have to be a great motivator, you have to be very good at praising and looking for the best in people. People are no different from flowers. If you water flowers, they flourish. If you praise people, they flourish. That's a critical attribute of a leader."

Richard's score: 9 out of 10

Professional Will

A performance catalyst

Few Leaders in the world push their team to be the best like Richard does. This is unarguably, one of Richard's finest trait. A collection of his quotes aggregated on kissmetrics.com lists the various ways in which Richard advises and pushes people to Dream big and be the best.

Richard says in his book 'Losing my virginity,' "Because I sometimes think in life you've got to dream big by setting yourself seemingly impossible challenges. You then have to catch up with them. You can make what people believe is impossible possible if you set big enough targets. Flying from New York to Australia in, say, two hours. Can we do it in our lifetimes? I'm determined to try. If you don't dream, nothing happens. And we like to dream big."

Richard's score: 10 out of 10

Builds for the long term

Virgin Blue was launched on August 31, 2000 with A$10 million. Virgin Blue introduced one-way fares from Brisbane to Sydney for under A$100 while Qantas-Ansett, the mega duopoly, were charging A$150. With such aggressive pricing and operational excellence, Virgin Blue started taking market share away from the old duopoly.

In June 2001, Singapore airlines, which had a stake in New Zealand air, which in turn had a stake in Ansett, made an unsolicited take over offer for A$250million to Virgin Blue to make them go away.

Per his account in his book: 'Business Stripped Bare', Richard Branson chose against the short term 25 time gain in favor of building a better airline and bringing better value to Australian customers. By December 2003, Virgin Blue's market cap on the ASX was A$2.3 billion, providing employment to over 4200 people.

Richard's score: 10 out of 10

Does whatever it takes

Richard does everything possible, both personally and professionally, to ensure the long term success of the Virgin group. With slim marketing budgets, Richard regularly puts aside his personal status and throws himself in front of the media dressed as whatever to save marketing expenses for a new venture.

Also, as previously noted, Richard postponed 25x return in a year on his investment in Virgin Blue to focus on the longer term and build a bigger, stronger and better company. This part is definitely easier said than done.

Also, Richard eats the humble pie regularly by accepting failures in ventures, when it gets harder to win, in the interest of conserving resources for the longer term.

Richard's score: 9 out of 10

Takes blame for poor results

Branson launched Virgin Cola in 1994. A number of factors went wrong and the venture did not do well. However, whenever he talked about Virgin cola Richard accepted this failure as simply his own failure and did not resort to assigning the blame to economic factors or his team. He said:

"That business taught me not to underestimate the power of the world's leading soft drink makers. I'll never again make the mistake of thinking that all large, dominant companies are sleepy!"

Richard's score: 8/10

Final Analysis

Richard scored 69 out of 80, which is approximately 86%. While there might be some subjectivity in our analysis, we can reasonably state the Richard comes pretty close to being a Level 5 leader. We must, however, regard that Richard is an exceptional leader and probably ranks better than most Level 4 leaders, but, because of the flamboyance aspect, falls short of a Level 5 leader.

RECAP

In this chapter, we explored the importance of ethics to becoming a globally effective leader and using these principles behind effective leadership to manage organizations at any scale. We first looked at the dark side of leadership by looking at the traits, vices and social factors that reduce our leadership capabilities. Next, we looked at what leaders do and what leaders should do. Finally, we looked at the principles of Level 5 leadership by stacking up Sir Branson against what it takes to be a true level 5 leader.

ACTION ITEM

Check out the blank template of Level 5 leadership. Critically and honestly analyze yourself against the Level 5 traits to see how you do. It is ok you don't do well. Trust me, I suck on it. The best part is that, like me, you will find areas that you can improve on.

CHAPTER THREE

LEADING NEGOTIATIONS

The greatest ability in business is to get along with others and influence their actions.

- John Hancock

This is a true police case. In the dead of the night around 1 am, three unidentified men enter a house on 22 Norwich Ave in Providence Rhode Island looking for drugs and cash. Residents panic and call 911, but the invaders immediately hang the call up. They search, find nothing and begin to violently question the residents. They take the innocent family hostage. Among the family is an 8 year old boy. Police arrive the scene. The suspects are armed, angry, and violent. The mother is pleading the invaders to spare the life of her family. Everything depends on Sgt. Michael Wheeler, the hostage negotiator assigned to handle the situation. Whatever Wheeler does will decide the fate of the child, the family, and the numerous police officers at the scene. If you are Sgt. Michael Wheeler, what do you do? This is one of the toughest situations to be in. Stick with me. We will develop a systematic way to handle this situation or for that matter, any type of negotiation.

Leaders influence. Leaders inspire. Leaders convince. Leaders persuade. Leaders coerce gently. Great Leaders are excellent negotiators. Accordingly, it is imperative that we master this area. There is an overwhelming amount of matter out there on negotiations. There is also a ton of research out there. Most of it is disorganized. And, they all seem to be be saying the same thing in different words. Nothing really did it for me. So, I chose to focus on professionals who do this for a living in very high pressure, very high stakes situations: Hostage negotiators. That is correct. We will use hostage negotiation techniques for business negotiations. We will learn from the best in the field who deal with stakes significantly higher than most billion dollars businesses will ever do — Matters of life and death involving kidnapped kids, families, hostages in botched robberies, armed barricades and suicide interventions.

Does this shit really work? You bet. According to John Flood, who is head of the FBI Negotiation unit, less than one in five incidents are resolved strictly through tactical means. The rest are made easy, peaceful and involve significantly less use of force because of the persuasive power of skilled negotiations. In fact, 95% of the situations end peacefully without any fatalities thanks in huge part to skilled negotiators.

WHAT IS WRONG WITH BUSINESS NEGOTIATIONS TODAY

Everything is negotiable. Whether or not the negotiation is easy is another thing.

- Carrie Fisher, "Princess Leia", Star Wars

Businesses are rational while humans are emotional. That's it. It makes sense to conduct all areas of our business rationally. So when it comes to negotiating a business contract, resolving industrial dispute or conflict, or even laying off the employee who served the company for 35 years, we do the same thing: approach rationally. And, it fails miserably in most situations.

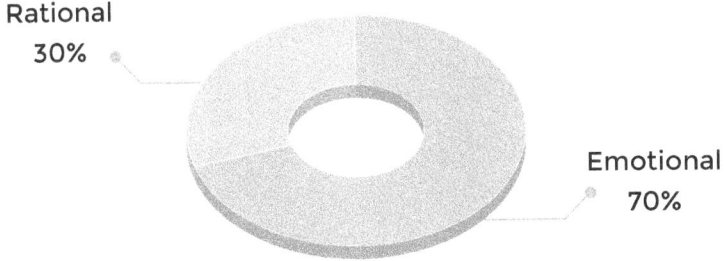

Weight of emotions in negotiations

Stating "I can prove with numbers and facts that you are wrong and I am right," would work if people were completely rational. But that is not the case. Roughly 70% of our decision making is influenced by our emotional side and only 30% by rational side. It gets even worse when we are filled with emotions. The rational side is completely shutoff and our decisions making is entirely based in emotions.

Moreover, owing to the existence of legal system and case law, and an easy alternative to just "turn this over to the lawyers," most business negotiations pretend that emotions don't exist. And, that makes things harder or leads to avoidable legal expenses.

This is why it is important to approach negotiations with an emotional angle and first defuse any negative emotions and sow the seeds of positive emotions, if we are to have any decent chance of generating the outcome we desire. The emotional side is so important that FBI's hostage negotiation unit came up with the Behavioral Change Stairway Model which goes as follows:

- Active Listening: Listen to their side and let them know you are listening. Get to know them.
- Empathy: Acquire an understanding of their emotional state and where they're coming from. Gather information.
- Build Rapport: Let them know that you understand their feelings. Once they are convinced that you understand their feelings, they will start to trust you.
- Influence: One you have gained their trust, they will let you work with them on the problem they are facing. You can now suggest alternative course of actions.

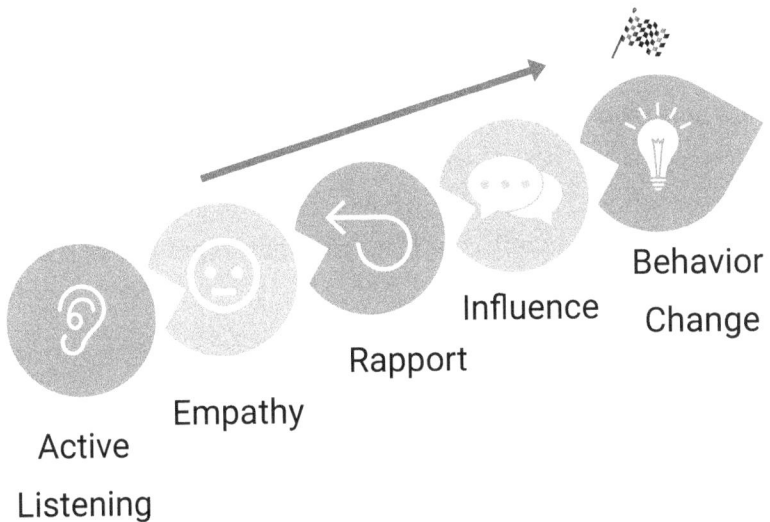

Stairway model of Hostage Negotiations

- Voluntary Behavioral Change: Use persuasion, backed by information gathered earlier to persuade them to do the right thing or take the action you want them to take.

Initially, these techniques were used to just buy time from the criminal holding a hostage so that the SWAT team had a chance to understand the environment and deploy. But, lately it has been discovered that these techniques are so powerful that use of force is not needed at all. That is the power of addressing emotions. If you notice, the first three are about addressing the emotional side and last two step are about rational bargaining. Unfortunately, in business negotiations, most people skip the steps 1-3 and start at step 4 and 5. There really is no foreplay. They skip straight to it. Doesn't work in lovemaking. Doesn't work in negotiations. The behavior of terrorist, hostage takers or invaders defies logic, as they usually do not care for their own safety or that of others. It is hard to negotiate with someone who doesn't care about their life. But, everyone cares about something. There is a reason they got out of bed, out on their clothes and are here in an inclement situation risking getting shot, instead of just swallowing a cyanide pill and having a relatively peaceful death. Everyone cares about something. This is universally true. True even in business. So, one of the prime objective of the first three phases is to gather info and find out what they care about. Because, this will be your leverage. This is the carrot you will be able to wield in front of them to get the outcome you desire.

BASICS OF NEGOTIATIONS

Let us first cover some generic concepts to get you up to speed. Negotiations are needed in any scenario where there are disagreement between parties. These disagreements can take the following forms.

- **Problems** are an existence of difference between what was expected by one party and what was delivered by the other. For e.g. if the pool was supposed to be rectangular but the contractor built a bean shaped pool, there is a problem.
- **Grievances** occur when a party feels that they have been wronged, injured, or there has been unjustly treated by the other party.
- **Disputes** are based on short term disagreements and usually involve issues that can be reasonably solved over negotiations. Disagreements over the sale price of car or a real estate are disputes. Disputes involve less emotions and are more about the primary metric in the transaction, where each side is trying to increase the net benefit, usually at the cost of the other.

Variants of Disagreements

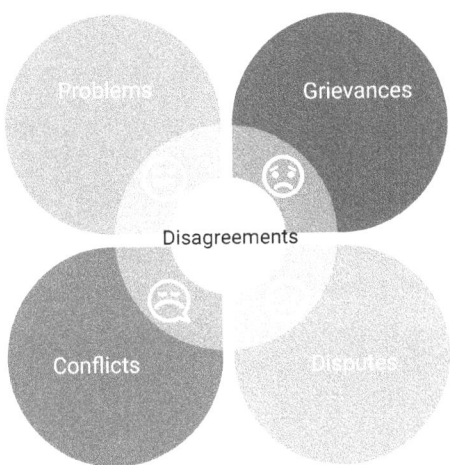

- **Conflicts** stem from long term, deeply rooted disagreements that have not been addressed in time. If disputes are left unresolved, they plants themselves on either sides and turn into conflicts. Conflicts usually involve significant anger and emotion on either sides.

Problems, grievances, disputes and conflicts lead to disagreements. Naturally, the purpose of a negotiation is to remove the disagreements and bring the parties to a mutual agreement.

No problem is so deep that it cannot be overcome, given the will of all parties, through discussion and negotiation rather than force and violence.

- Nelson Mandela

Position versus Interests

Position is whatever a party is demanding. Interest is what they actually want. Interest is the underlying reason why a party is demanding whatever it is that they are demanding. When negotiations start, the interests and positions of the each party will differ. During the course of negotiation, the positions and interests will come closer (if the negotiation is working) or shift further apart (if the negotiation is not working). Towards the end of a successful negotiation, the positions and interests will usually be the closest possible, given the equilibrium of needs and wants on either sides.

Stances in Negotiations

If the parties are focussing only on what they want, they are said to be engaged in a **Distributive negotiation**. Each side is thinking about just distributing whatever value is available to claim. They are looking at this as a win-lost situation. They can only win if the other party loses. They think that they can only get 60% of the pie if the other gets 40%. Each commit to a position early in the process and think only of their own wants and needs. It is an adversarial method of bargaining and pits the parties against one another.

On the other hand, if the parties are thinking about how both parties can arrive at a mutually beneficial outcome, they are said to be engaged in an **Integrative negotiation**. Parties are thinking about how they can expand the pie and then get an equitable share of the pie.

Let's take a classic example of two girls fighting over an orange. Both girls take the **position** that they want the whole orange. Their mother cuts the orange in half and gives each girl one half. This outcome represents a compromise. But, it isn't the best one, because it is a distributive negotiation. If the mother had asked the girls why they wanted the orange there could have been a better outcome. This is because one girl wanted to drink orange juice, while the other just wanted the peel so that she could use them in baking some orange flavored cookies. If their mother had resorted to integrative negotiation and enquired about their **interests**, they could have both gotten all of what they wanted, rather than just half. Let's take a more modern example. Select Electric Vehicle (EV) makers like Tesla, Jaguar, Nissan should form a cooperative cartel to install a dense global network of superchargers. And, they should make sure that these charges are at every gas station and location in between. This will overcome the biggest hurdle to owning all electric vehicles: mileage/range anxiety. This will increase sales of the EVs category by taking away share from gas powered incumbents. EVs can fight with each other for individual market share. Overtime, this network could turn into an entry barrier or this cartel can license the network per use to new entrants creating valuable revenue stream.

As unbelievable as it may sound, sometimes, the parties just don't know what they want. Or, what they can get out of the transaction. So, they take an absurd position and usually stick to this position out of ego till the very end and usually end up with nothing.

Sometimes, the parties know what their interests are, but they will take a different position just to mislead the other party. Skilled negotiators can sniff out the interest by just making the parties talk during active listening.

> *Every day's a negotiation and sometimes it's done with guns.*
> - Joss Whedon, American Producer

At other times they just want to hurt the other party at all costs. Yes, it happens all the time. A party may take a position that can only result in self-harm only because taking that position is the only way for them to cause serious harm to the other party. Suicide bombers are very strong examples of this. In Sri Lanka, the Liberation Tigers of Tamil Eelam (LTTE), a secular guerrilla movement, began using suicide bombers in the late 1980s, as part of their campaign to create a separate state for Tamil people in Northern and Eastern Sri Lanka. They called these suicide bombers, Black Tigers. The Black Tigers led the world in suicide terrorism from 1980 to 2003. Time Magazine describe the LTTE as 'the most successful terrorist organization in the world.' Of the 137 suicide bombings carried out by the LTTE, two were high profile assassinations: the Sri Lankan Prime Minister, Ranasinghe Premadasa, and the Indian Prime Minister, Rajiv Gandhi. The Black Tigers also invented the suicide belt which would be used regularly in Iraq, Afghanistan and

Pakistan. Every time a Black Tiger adorns the belt, they are taking a position in which they will pay the ultimate price: The loss of their life only to cause a loss of life of a much more important figure of the opposite party. Can you think of another example where one party wants to hurt the other at all costs? Acrimonious divorce. If a husband cheats on his wife, the aggrieved wife will drag the husband along in a long drawn out divorce proceeding which will usually end up with two very wealthy divorce lawyers. Think I am kidding? I won't bore you with three or four year long celebrity divorces here. Nicholas Purpura, 62, a powerful executive from the now defunct Bear Stearns, and his ex-wife Barbara loved divorcing each other so much that they made the experience last almost two decades. The couple had been legally divorced since 1988, but the battle spanned thousands of hours of courtroom testimony spread over a good 18 years. Barbara sued him for abandonment, and he countersued for "cruel and inhumane treatment," which involves accusing her of "humiliating and demeaning" him, and calling him a "bozo" in front of the kids. The battle lasted so long that four of the dozens of jurists who heard the evidence died before the divorce could be finalized.

Apart from the obvious loss of value in a distributive transaction, sketchy lawyers and preying mediators can be the next biggest cost item. Let me tell you the story of monkey bread. Two monkeys found a loaf a bread on the side of road. They started fighting over who should get a bigger share. "I saw the bread first. I should get it all" said Monkey 1. Monkey 2 snaps back a reply: "In your dreams, pal. Last week, I saw Beyonce in Central Park. Do I get to marry her? Hell no. Because, this handsome dude called Jay-Z grabbed her first. In the same way, I grabbed the bread first. I should get it all. Capishe?". Monkey 1 gets all emotional and says, "Really dude? You had to bring Beyonce up. You know I have a crush on her the size of Texas". They monkeys kept dueling verbally. Mr. Fox, who was chilling nearby, heard the two. "Easy Fellas. Allow me," Mr. Fox said unleashing a weighing scale. "I can divide the bread into equal halves. You fellas cool with that?". The monkeys agreed to his suggestion (Note: they agreed to this only because this obvious suggestion was coming from a neutral third party. Happens all the time). Mr. Fox, tears the bread into two using a bread knife and weighs the halves. One half is slightly heavier that the other and both monkeys want that heavier half. So, Mr. Fox tears a small piece of bread from the heavier half and eats it. Now the other half is heavier because Mr. Fox bit off too much. Both monkeys want this heavier one now. Again, Mr. Fox bites off a small piece from the heavier half and eats it. He bits off a little bit too much . This continues and eventually, bite by bite, Mr. Fox eats the whole bread, leaving the poor monkeys with nothing. Moral: Mediators will be the only beneficiaries if they see that the parties are fighting and aren't considering mutual interests as part of an integrative negotiation. In long term distributive negotiations, there is only one winner: the lawyers. Both parties will lose on account of litigation expenses.

RESOLVING DISAGREEMENTS

Disagreements with other parties can be resolved in three ways:

- By negotiating with them and finding a common ground between **Interests**.
- By using your **Rights** over them.
- By using your **Power** over them.

Use of negotiation should always be the preferred over using rights or power. You should use your rights or power over someone if they are unwilling to negotiate or if your discussions with them has reached an impasse. You might also be forced to use your rights or power if they are not acting in accordance with a mutual agreement. When you are going to use your rights or power, you are make it clear that the current behavior is not acceptable and that you will not be taken advantage of.

When you are forced to use your rights over them, you fall back to enforcing contracts or using legal remedies or invoke the use of traditions, customs or practice.

When you use power, you must deliver the threat without getting personal. When you make threats, be sure that you are threatening their interests and not their positions. You can say, "If you don't do X, I will be forced to do Y." In other situations, you might be required to say, "This is my last offer. Take it or leave it" or "This is non negotiable." It is wise to give the other party a chance to save face. You can say, "If you do Y, I can do Z." If they don't do X, you must then follow through on the threats. Follow through is important to establish credibility, especially in situations where there will be repeated future interactions e.g. dealing with family or with a key employee who is acting badly.

PREPPING FOR NEGOTIATION

Negotiation involves separating the people from the problems and separating positions from interests and then finding a common ground where parties agree to the best of their interests. Luck favors the prepared. Here are the areas you must focus on as part of preparation:

- BATNA is short for Best Alternative to a Negotiated Agreement. If you can develop multiple alternatives, you've for a great head-start.

- Target is the what you want to achieve in the negotiation. This is the most favorable outcome you can hope for. If you are selling a condo, this is the amount of money you would be happy to receive for it.

- RP is short for Reserve Price. This is the least favorable point at which you will accept a negotiated agreement. If you are selling a condo, this is the lowest amount of money for which you would sell it.
- ZOPA is short for Zone of Possible Agreement. Obviously, ZOPA is the range between Target and RP. Recognize if you are emotionally charged in this negotiation and find a way to defuse these emotions.
- Recognize if the other party is emotionally charged in this negotiation and developing a plan for how you will defuse these emotions.

- Recognize what your interests are and the position you will take at the beginning of the negotiation. Prepare solid and reasonable arguments for the position you will take.
- Recognize what the opposing interests are and the position they are likely to take at the beginning of the negotiation. It is ok to not know everything here. Prepare various hypotheses regarding what the other party might wants, and focus on testing these hypotheses during the negotiations.
- Are you going to negotiate yourself or negotiate through an Agent?
- Are you going to negotiate alone or negotiate as a team?
- Are there cross cultural issues you must be aware of?
- Is this a multi-party negotiation?

Before you walk into a negotiation, be prepared to fail. Failure means you will not get what you want. Walk in with a clear proposal as to what you are looking to obtain or achieve and be able to justify those requests. Being well prepared, will enable you to make clear arguments will significantly decrease the likelihood that you walk away with quite a bit less than what you wanted. It will also better enable you to "stick to your guns."

In addition to being prepared with solid arguments, you may also need to be prepared to walk away from the negotiating table. Your BATNA will be of immense help here and in most cases force the other party to soften the hard initial stance they have taken. Be ready to expect surprises in negotiations and don't stay fixated on your initial assumptions.

Teams and Agents

In one-off transactions like real estate or lawsuits, it is wise to use agents especially if the stakes are high. Agents are like double edged sword. There are pros and there are cons. Agents bring valuable negotiation expertise to the table and can help provide the detachment in cases where you cannot reliably manage your emotions. Unfortunately, agents can have agendas of their own that can run counter to your interests. A lawyer who charges by the hour has incentive to drag out the litigation. Real estate agents who deal with each other regularly can start bonding and can start striking higher priced deals simply because their commission is a proportion of the sale price. Accordingly, it is important to incentivize the agent correctly and possibly include a bonus in their compensation, if the outcome is favorable. It is also possible to fire the agent to save face in a negotiation that has reached an impasse.

Another important thing to be aware of: No matter how tough you think you are, you will be outnumbered when negotiating against a team. Literally. Don't attempt to go it alone against a team. Hire a lawyer or a professional mediator to be on your side. Detectives use this technique. You will mostly find two detectives interrogating a serial killer. While one detective is talking, the other will be carefully watching the suspect for non verbal cues. And, information gathered from these cues will be used to guide the course of interrogation. In high pressure situation, a team has a special advantage. The pressure is distributed over the team members. Moreover, teams are able to take a break, discuss courses of action and use each other a sounding board for ideas. Negotiating in teams can also be a double edged sword especially in corporate settings. Preparation is crucial in case of teams. There needs to be agreement on who will lead the negotiations, who will talk when and who is allowed to disclose how much information.

Teams can be an effective only if team members are able to uncover, leverage, and efficiently coordinate their diverse abilities.

Cultural nuances in negotiations

If you are leading or working for a global company, you will need to be aware of cultural issues in negotiations. Germans are generally punctual, Latins are habitually late, Japanese negotiate slowly, and Americans are quick to make a deal. Before going big and then going bust, when Enron was only a pipeline company, it lost a major contract in India because local authorities felt that it was pushing negotiations too fast. Academia maintains that there are two main types of cultures:

- Individualist cultures where people are more independent and competitive. They do not accept the poor circumstances and fight to improve them. Western cultures are usually more individualistic.
- Collectivists cultures where people are cooperative and interdependent. They accept the prevailing circumstance and adjust to their conditions. Asian cultures are generally more collectivists.

Some cultures are more formal than others. Germans have a more formal style than Americans. Germans generally insist on addressing others by their titles, avoids personal remarks, and refrains from questions pertaining to the private or family life. It is generally safer to adopt a formal stance and move to an informal stance, if the situation warrants it, rather than start an informal style and risk looking like a leader who is unaware of cultural nuances. Some cultures are direct while others are indirect. Japanese culture is more indirect than American. The indirect ways in which Japanese express disapproval have often led western executives to believe that their proposal still had a chance when in fact the Japanese executives had rejected them. Latin Americans show their emotions at the negotiating table, while the Japanese and many other Asians hide their feelings. Americans prefer detailed contracts that attempt to anticipate all possible circumstances. Why? Because the deal is the contract itself, and one must refer to the contract to handle new situations that may arise. Other cultures, such as the Chinese, prefer a contract in the form of general principles rather than detailed rules. Why? Because, Chinese culturally believe that the essence of the deal is the relationship between the parties. If unexpected circumstances arise, the parties fallback primarily on their relationship, not the contract, to solve the problem. Cultures also differ in how they structure a negotiation. Americans tend to favor the building-down approach, while the Japanese tend to prefer the building-up approach. In the building down approach, the one party begins by presenting the maximum deal and works to pare down the items that the other side does not agree to. In the building-up approach, the process begins by putting minimum deal on the table and then items are added as the other party accepts additional conditions. Western cultures typically favor individual decision making while eastern cultures favor group decision making. In major deals, Americans to arrive at the table with three people and while the Chinese show up with ten. The best way to deal with a culture that you are not too familiar with is to find out how to pay respect in that culture and set a standard for how much you are willing to change. As a smart leader, you must make a conscious attempt to avoid ethnocentrism, which means evaluating other cultures according to preconceptions originating in the standards and customs of your own culture.

How to invite a party to negotiation

Never invite anyone to negotiate. Just invite them to talk. You can say, "Let's put our heads together and figure out a solution". Or, "Let's brainstorm some ideas together". Or, "Let's work on this problem together". A hospital asking a physician whether or not they wish to continue practice at the hospital for the next few years is an invitation for negotiation. If the physician indicated that he would like to continue, then a formal offer could be made, which would begin the process of negotiation for the contractual salary. Did you know that purchasing departments routinely prepare an invitation to negotiate or an ITN? An ITN is simply a competitive solicitation for goods or services along with a listing of whether/if factors other than price are to be considered in the contract assignment. Similarly, newspaper advertisements, price quotations, and catalog prices are all invitations to negotiate.

I am never going to say that inviting someone to negotiate who is ignoring you or just won't respond to you is easy. The trick here is to frame our invitation into a question that calls upon their moral values. If a your girlfriend is angry because you missed a lunch-movie date because you were too hungover from the night out with the boys and she is completely ignoring repeated calls and texts from you, do this. Observe complete silence for two days. This will leave her wondering, clear the slate in her mind, and make her want for communication. Then write, "Have you completely given up on us?" or "Have you completely given up on hopes of us being a happy couple forever?". She will respond with a No.

Negotiating a deal can only take place when there are two parties. If you wait too long, the other party may already have negotiated a deal with someone else.

Robert Irwin, Historian & Writer

If a prospect has gone cold, after several days of responsive discussion, you could write, "Have you given up on working with me to develop a good solution for your company?". The prospect will respond with a No. Are you seeing a pattern emerge here?

Seasoned hostage negotiator Chris Voss maintains that the word "no" has immense power. Chris has done fantastic work to advance the art and science of negotiation and I don't think he is getting the credit he deserves. Chris states that many times people will say no in a negotiation because doing so makes them feel safe and in control. Expert negotiators know that a "no" is the start of the negotiation, not the end of it. By letting them say no at the beginning of the conversation, you're letting them feel like they are making the decisions and driving the conversation.

> *Persuasion is not about how bright or smooth or forceful you are. It's about the other party convincing themselves that the solution that you want is their own idea.*
>
> - Chris Voss, Seasoned hostage negotiator

It actually starts the conversation and gives them the safety and comfort they need to get to a real "yes." In fact, sometimes the only way to get the other person to truly listen to you is to let them get that initial "no" out of their system! After that initial "no," put forward questions like:

- "Will you help me understand which part of this proposal doesn't work for you?"

- "What can we do together to make this work for you?"

"It seems like there is something here that bothers you. Would you like to share it with me."

They will reply and often, you will hear the information you need to get them to a real yes. See, you went from being ignored to back and forth negotiation. Smooth, isn't it?

RECAP

In this chapter, we discussed the scientific art of negotiation its central importance in any leadership role. We first looked at the importance of human emotions in negotiations. Then, we looked at the different types of disagreements and ways to resolve disagreements by using right, power or negotiating based on interests. We explored the basics of negotiations and covered the cultural nuances that can affect negotiations. Finally, we looked at how to prepare for negotiation and how to invite a party to negotiation. We will continue negotiations in the next chapter by learning how to execute business negotiations like a hostage negotiators.

ACTION ITEM

Think back to the last time you were in a negotiation. Now try to answer the following questions:

- Did you address the emotional elements first?
- Did you pay attention to the cultural nuances?

- How well did you prepare for the negotiations?
- How did you invite the other party to negotiations?

Finally, think about what would you have done differently knowing what you know now. This self reflection should be done after any negotiation. It is one of the most effective ways to learn about your personal weaknesses in stressful situations and get better at handling them next time.

CHAPTER FOUR

NEGOTIATING LIKE A HOSTAGE NEGOTIATOR

> *If there is negotiation, it must be rooted in mutual respect and concern for the rights of others.*
>
> - John F. Kennedy

Imagine a deep lake. You are one side. The opposing party is on the other side. The more emotional the issue, the deeper and wider the lake is. This is essentially what most negotiations looks like. So, the first objective of any negotiation should be to **defuse emotions** and build a bridge of positive emotions so that our words can travel to the other side exactly as we intended. Failing that everything we say can and will be misunderstood. Can someone deaf hear what you are saying? Nope. They just don't have the ability to hear. Similarly, the opposing party have the ability to hear, but they have no ear for what you are going to tell them. Because they will filter everything you say and modify it and then interpret it. We use context to interpret. And, what we think about the speaker, affects our interpretation to a great extent.

Empathizing Effectively

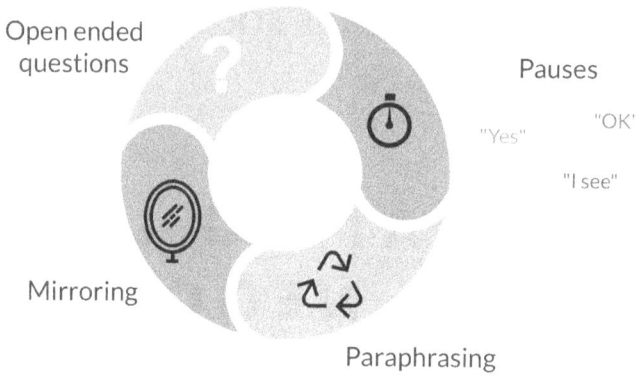

And, if they think negatively about us, they are going to take negatively whatever we say. We will not get the benefit of doubt. If we don't have a bridge of positive emotions with the other side, we have not earned the right to work on the problem with them. We must change the way they think and see us. If we can change how they view us, we can change what they hear. So, how do you defuse negative emotions? Allowing the other side to speak first and listening actively is one of the best ways to defuse negative emotions.

NEGOTIATING LIKE A HOSTAGE NEGOTIATOR

Most people address conflicts or disputes by taking the middle ground. Never do that. Expert negotiation is about finding leverage in any situation and securing the best possible deal, while being fair to all parties involved. So the first and foremost advise in any negotiation is to start with a good heart and an inclination to do the right thing. Without the goodness in your heart to do the right thing, you will find it extremely difficult to do the second (empathize) and third steps (build rapport) correctly and succeed in securing the best deal possible for everyone involved. When you are doing the right thing and doing right by people, the universe will line up to help you out. Things will start falling in place. The gambles you take along the way will work in your favor.

How to Listen Actively

Active listening is the key to the next two steps of empathy and building rapport. It involves letting the other guy have the airtime and making them feel like they are being heard. Think about this, when you first meet at the negotiation table, there is only disagreement or conflict, no relationship. But, as soon as you let them speak and start listening, you are already in a cooperative, complying relationship of speaker and listener. They are speaking. You are listening. That is a step forward from where you were when you first sat down at the negotiation table. An excellent side effect of this is that you will collect information that you didn't have before. We psychologically bond with people who listen to us. It is the whole works. Their eyes focussed on us, their face pointed in our direction. It is almost like by listening we are giving the other person the floor to speak and convey their side. It is sort of giving them something as a token of good faith. Like extending the first friendly hand. Whether they realize it or not consciously, but subconsciously they will realize that you have given them something. The airtime belongs to both of you, but you let them have it first. This is the first step to have them like you. The objective of active listening is to have them move from not liking you to liking you. While they are speaking, postpone any urge to interrupt, disagree, evaluate or

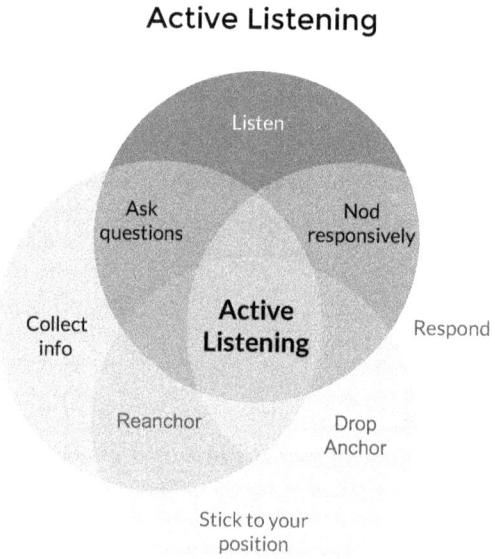

judge.

Chris Voss advises: "If while you're making your argument, the only time the other side is silent is because they're thinking about their own argument, they've got a voice in their head that's talking to them. They're not listening to you. When they're making their argument to you, you're thinking about your argument, that's the voice in your head that's talking to you. So it's very much like dealing with a schizophrenic. Hear the other side out, that's the only way you can quiet the voice in the other guy's mind. Active listening sets the stage for genuine empathy.

One exception to the rule of allowing the other party to speak first is in a case where the dispute is not emotional and just based on disagreement on numbers. Here, you must make a demand way higher than your target price. This is called **Dropping an anchor**. Don't be afraid to come out of the gate with a number that is twice or three times the number you are looking for, provided you are fully aware that they are extreme and you most likely will not get them. The strategy behind this being that it is much easier to start at the top and work your down to a mutually beneficial agreement. This is way easier than starting low and trying to work your way up the negotiating table. If the opponent is skilled and tries to drop and anchor of unreasonable demand, you must immediately state the price you are willing to pay which is way lower than the price you are comfortably willing to pay. This is called **Re-anchoring**.

How to Empathize effectively

Sympathy is feeling compassion, sorrow, or pity for the hardships that another person encounters. Empathy is the experience of understanding another person's thoughts, feelings, and condition from his or her point of view, rather than from one's own. Empathy facilitates prosocial or helping behaviors that come from within, rather than being forced, so that people behave in a more compassionate manner.

Here are some more things to empathize with the other party and create a platform for building rapport:

- Ask open ended questions. Not questions that have one word answers. This is the corner stone of empathy.
- Be calm and use pauses to encourage them to keep talking or to defuse emotions. You can say, "Yes," "O.K.," or "I see."

Asking Open Ended Questions

Close ended question	Response	Correct open ended question
How are you doing?	Good	How are you feeling about the situation with
Do you have need for our service	No	If we were to work together, what are the top two outcomes you would like to see?
Can you sign a 2 year deal?	Nope	What terms are you most flexible with?
Will you be able sign a contract this year?	No Sir	What would stop you from signing this year when we give you a 25% discount?

- Repeat the last word person said to show you're listening and engaged. People like it when you repeat words they have just uttered. This technique is called mirroring. When we are talking to friends, we subconsciously mirror them, mimicking body language and enthusiasm, and showing we are at ease. But, naturally, we don't do this with someone we don't consider a friend. In negotiation, we just need to use the same mirroring technique to get into that natural mode of friendly conversation and invite/pull the other party into a friendly, collaborative state of mind.

- You can also repeat what the person said back to them in your own words. By doing this, you show that you truly understand what they are saying and aren't merely repeating. This technique is called paraphrasing.

While following the advice here, be sure to let your instincts guide you on the speed and flow of the process. You have six amazing senses and you come pre-equipped to judge how well it is going. Don't try to rush the process or fake it. Fake empathy is very evident and will significantly compromise your credibility in a negotiation.

If you are planning on doing business with someone again, don't be too tough in the negotiations. If you're going to skin a cat, don't keep it as a house cat.

- Marvin S. Levin, Author & Businessman

How to build Rapport

Rapport is a harmonious relationship in which the people understand each other's feelings or ideas and communicate well. When you have a rapport with someone, you're better placed to influence them and they are more likely to accept your ideas, to share information, and to create opportunities together. This makes rapport a must-have in any negotiation before any fruitful negotiation can begin. Without active listening and genuine empathy, building a good rapport is impossible.

Building a rapport in situations where emotions are running high starts with active listening, and continues with mirroring and paraphrasing. Be culturally appropriate, relaxed, hold your head up, maintain a good posture. If you feel at anytime, the other party is drifting away from you, take a break. **Breaks** are an effective tool in doing redirection. In fact, ask them to take a walk with you or go grab coffee. Even if they say no, it will install a sliver of guilt in them for rejecting you and this guilt will help you out later.

> *Negotiation is all about building trust, removing suspicion and developing a sense of mutual confidence in the other party.*
>
> - Richard Ellis, Executive, CBRE

To build a good rapport, use the information you collected during the active listening phase to find **common grounds**. This could be as simple as frustration with the traffic in the city or the excessively high rate of parking in the downtown garages. It could be growing up in a same area or going to same school district or rooting for the same sport teams. Use everyday language. Feel free to use normal everyday expletives like "darn it," "eff it," or "crap". In business settings, shared experiences create a great platform for building good rapport. This is the reason people go to trade shows and conferences.

Once the party starts expressing their emotions by saying things like, "I am tired of life," "I am frustrated," or "I have always been stomped on," label their feelings to show that you identify and confirm the emotions expressed by them. This technique is called **Emotional Labeling**. Don't comment on the validity of the feelings. Because that will make them feel like they are being judged. You CANNOT say, "You don't need to feel that way. If they fired you, they are not worth your time." Saying this minimizes their feelings. And, their feelings are a major part of why they are in this situation. It is better not to risk opening that can of worms. You can say, "You sound pretty hurt about being fired. It doesn't seem fair."

How to Influence like an expert

Once you have established a rapport with the opposing party, you can with them on coming up with different ways to solve the issues on the table. Make all attempts to share information with the other party and see if they are sharing information back. This exchange of information will enable both of you to understand the issues better and come up creative solutions to the problems at hand, where you could both win. You will have to use the rapport and be subtle in influencing the party. You want to stay on the course of doing the right thing for yourself and for them, but to make it easier on yourself, you will need to give them an illusion of control and make them feel that they are coming up with the various courses of action. You want to set the stage for effecting a voluntary behavioral change. You want to nudge them and steer them to reach the solution you want, making them think it is their solution.

Firstly, exuding confidence is extremely important in this phase. **Use silence effectively** to communicate confidence. Ask your question and keep mum. Yes, it may seem awkward, but it will remarkably improve your position. If the customer sends you an offer via email or voice-mail, don't be in a hurry to respond. Just wait and remain silent. Quite often, the other person will take your silence as rejection and in turn sweeten the deal for you.

Negotiating Like a Hostage Negotiator

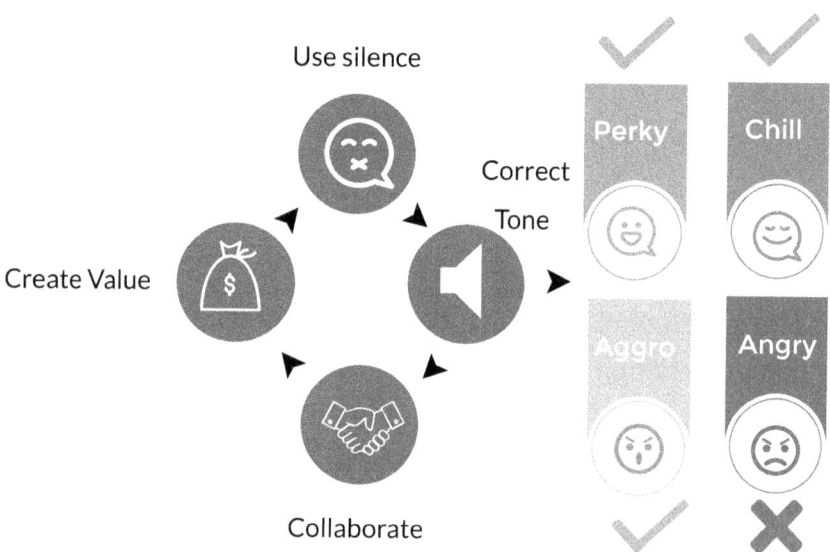

Next, using the **right tone of voice** is paramount. What is common about the way in which Anthony Hopkins, Clint Eastwood, Morgan Freeman, Sean Connery speak? They all speak in lower tone of voice and are all well known for playing extremely strong characters that dominate the movies they are in. Morgan Freeman is chosen by casting when there is a need for a character with traits like sincerity and trustworthiness. There are three main types of voices you can use in negotiations and one that you should never use:

- Perky upbeat voice should be used to project the image of someone likable and comfortable in the current situation.
- Chill smooth-jazz voice should be deployed to project and image of authority, warmth and someone trustworthy. Use a downward voice inflection to indicate that you are in control when you are making a

point or indicate that something is non negotiable. Use an upward voice inflection to indicate openness and encouraging if you are asking an open ended question. Why is this important? People feel defensive when they are questioned. Using a downward inflection of voice will make them feel less threatened because when

- Aggressive assertive voice should only be used when your back is against the wall or you need to assert your rights to steer the negotiation that is getting out of your control. Assertive voice should sound firm, but not disrespectful. Promise yourself that you will not speak more than two sentences in a row in the aggressive voice. Because then you will be bordering on anger and loss of control. Moreover, this will only invite the other party to pushback. You can say assertively, "I don't think we are getting anywhere with this fighting" and then follow up with something that is down a notch like "I'll give you three minutes to get all the anger out, only if you promise me that you will work with me on sorting out the issues on the table after that."

- Angry yelling voice should never be used because it sounds desperate and indicates loss of control.

To be an effective negotiator, train yourself to slow down. Low, slow voices have the most influence. Not only can your audience understand you, they become invested in your point of view and are more likely to jump on board and do what you want them to do.

This is the point where you collaborate with other parties and focus on creating value. This means increasing the size of the pie, or in other words, increasing the total value up for grabs. Imagine that you and six other gladiators have just been dropped into the Roman Colosseum. You are to fight the other gladiators till only the last one is standing.

What do you do? Before the fight starts, each gladiator has a life equity of 1/6 (assuming all gladiators are almost nearly matched). If you could secretly persuade one other gladiator to team up with you (before the fight stats), then suddenly your combined life equity goes up to 2/6. Then, as a team you can isolate the others one by one, and fight and eradicate them until they are all gone. It will be easier since a team of two will be twice as strong as an individual gladiator. With two gladiators standing, your life equity has now gone up to 1/2. Both of you drastically improved your chances of winning the final battle from 1/6 to 1/2.

Let us apply the concept of creating value this to a more modern setting. Imagine three pizzerias at a busy city intersection. As owner of one of the pizzerias, you earn a third of the customer traffic. You know that profit = (revenue from selling pizza - costs of making the pizza) x number of pizza sold. One way to increase your profits is to advertise, bring in more customers, and sell more pizzas. But, the other two can also start advertising more. Your increased advertising will have no more effect and your money will be wasted. Then, the only one getting rich would be the advertising firm. There is another way to increase profits. Look at your costs. If you can convince the other pizzeria owners to buy pizza dough, cheese, mushrooms, meat, etc as a group, you will be able to negotiate a better bulk rate from the suppliers. Your costs will go down. This will be mutually beneficial because you are increasing the size of the pie here. Pun intended.

If you think this is baloney, regard that while Apple and Samsung compete fiercely on the smartphone front, Samsung supplies almost all the displays for the Apple iPhones. Huge companies fight on some fronts, while they collaborate on other fronts. They increase value where they can and claim value where necessary. It is entirely normal for a dozen lawsuits to be going on between two companies, while they are supplying each other numerous components or licensing technology from one another.

How to effect Voluntary Behavioral Change

Leadership is the art of getting someone else to do something you want done because he wants to do it.

- Dwight Eisenhower

Once you have succeeded in coming up with ways to solve the issues on the table, it is time to employ persuasive techniques to nudge them and steer them to reach the solution you want, making them think it is their solution. This is the stage in which you claim value for your side. **Share data and facts** and make arguments that are backed by these data and facts that persuade the other side to understand that you fairly deserve more than what you are asking for. If you can invoke this feeling for "you deserve it" in their minds, they will voluntarily take steps to give you the deal you are looking for.

In reaching a deal, you might need to give something up in order to get something. But, remember one iron rule: **No unilateral concessions**. You cannot give them anything without having them give you something in return. Making unilateral concessions seriously compromises your position and ability to secure any kind of deal out of people. Similarly, do not ask for unilateral concessions. They will say a flat no, and it will diminish your respect in the situation.

Effect Behavior Change

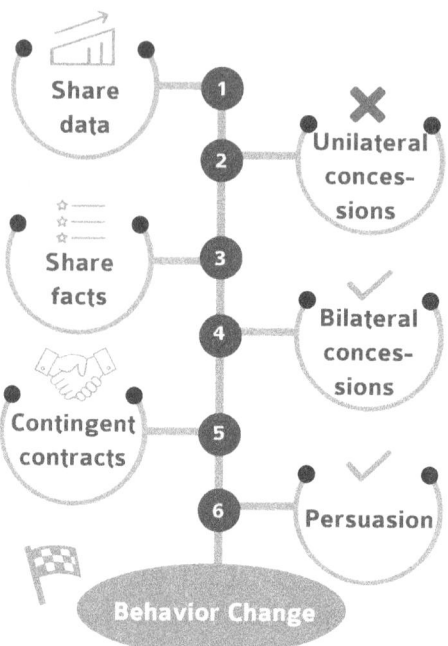

Let us assume that you are negotiating with a prospect and you want them to sign a 1-year deal. You must propose a 3-year program that you already know will be outside their comfort zone. When they say no to that offer, you can counter with the 1-year offer, which will suddenly look much more attractive. People are more satisfied with the outcome of a negotiation when there is some back and forth. For example, say you are going to buy a pre-owned car and the asking price is $50k. You make an offer of $40k. If the seller accepts it immediately, you will start wondering if you could have gotten a better deal if you had offered even lower, like $35k. But if the seller counters with $45k, and the two of you eventually settle on $42k, you will actually be more satisfied with the outcome than if there had been no back and forth negotiations, even though you ended up paying 2k more.

In the case of the customer who asks for a discount, you might say, "No, I can't offer you a reduced rate, but I can split it up into two payments…" or whatever terms would be agreeable to you. A variation on that is the no… but if… scenario. You can say, "No, I can't reduce my price, but if you are willing to commit to a longer contract, I could offer you first month free." This allows you to stand your ground on terms that are nonnegotiable, while still allowing you to also present an alternative that might be a win for the other party.

Keep your target in mind when making deals. Do not make deals that are outside your ZOPA. Remember, not every deal has to be made. Sometimes, it is better to walk away.

It's possible to get the deal you want, only to have the deal unfold later. People will sometimes agree to things they really don't plan on doing, simply to get out of a high pressure situation. As a negotiator, you must observe both verbal and non-verbal cues carefully, to make sure you have a real agreement that will be executed. You must make sure that there has been a meeting of minds.

Finally, if there are uncertainties or risks associated with implementing the mutual agreement, then it is smart to create contingent contracts. Few things are as unpredictable as teenagers these days. If you negotiate the norms of behavior with your teenager, it is important to include contingent contracts that covers the possible range of outcomes. The teenager agrees to behave well with siblings, stay out of trouble at school, complete homework in time, come back home before 8p. The teenager can keep their privileges contingent upon following the agreed upon norms (main agreement). If the teenager violates these rules, they will be grounded, lose their weekly allowance, and access to internet and television (Negative contingent contract). If the teenager gets straight As in the school year, they will get 50% raise in allowance (Positive contingent contract).

CLOSING OUT NEGOTIATIONS

After an agreement is reached, invite the other party to see how the negotiation could be improved.

If the negotiations fail, most of the times, it is clear why a deal was not reached. But if you not clear about why a deal did not happen, consider making a follow-up call. Even though you may not win the deal back in the end, you might learn something that's useful for next time. People are more willing to disclose the information if they don't think you're in a "selling" mode.

After the negotiation is completed, try to find time to reflect on what went down. Some questions you can ask are: What did I want from this negotiation? How close was I to walking away? Did I manage my emotions correctly? Did I get what I want or was I made to believe that this is what I wanted? This reflection will help you learn and make you a better negotiator and a better leader.

What did Sgt. Wheeler do?

Let's see how Sgt. Wheeler applied everything he knows about negotiations to the situation at hand. Wheeler is a 30 year veteran of the police force and a trained negotiator. Around 2:45am, Wheeler gets into the neighboring house, and begins communicating with the hostage takers. They demand at once: "We will leave as soon as the police leaves". (The invaders are surrounded by cops, but that doesn't stop them from making a bold ask.)

Wheeler immediately cut them off, "The police are not going anywhere". This is Re-anchoring. What is notable is that Wheeler did not lie to them. Remember, the FBI negotiation strategy says, only lie to someone if you are about to kill them. If Wheeler agreed to it quickly, he might have come across as untruthful. But, by being straight up, he established a credibility in this negotiation.

Over the next six long hours, Wheeler listened actively. He spoke with a firm but calm tone of voice. He responded with genuine inquisitiveness and empathy using non-judgmental words like "OK," "I hear ya," "This isn't the best of situations. But, let's work it out". "Time helps defuse all emotions. As long as they were talking to me, they weren't hurting anyone else," Wheeler said later in reports to Providence Journal. By listening actively, Wheeler gathered that they cared deeply about their families. Especially, one of them cared about his mother. Later, he discovered that another one cared about his 7-year old daughter. Eventually, Wheeler established a rapport with the invaders and gained their trust. So much that these men asked Wheeler for a pack of cigarettes. Wheeler gave them a few but only after they promised that they will release the 7 year old. Remember, no unilateral concessions. They smoked the cigarettes but did not keep their promise. Five long hours of back and forth and all Wheeler had to show for it was a broken promise. Instead of getting frustrated, Wheeler kept his calm and kept persuading them emotionally by leveraging the information he had gathered by listening actively. Wheeler appealed to him as a Father. "How would your daughter feel in this situation? Can you imagine how afraid she would be? Why don't you let the little boy out?". Finally, at 7:45 am, they released the boy. Wheeler offered them one more cigarette and kept persuading them to come out, promising safe arrest and appealing to their emotional familial side. In the end, around 9am, the men surrendered, bringing the 6 hour long standoff to a peaceful conclusion, made possible in large part to the power of skillful negotiations.

RECAP

In this chapter, we covered how to execute negotiations like a pro by learning from hostage negotiators. We did that by learning how to listen actively, empathize and build a rapport. Finally, we covered how to influence and persuade the other party to effect voluntary behavioral change.

ACTION ITEM

Dial back to the last time when you were in a negotiation. Apply everything we explored here to conduct a self reflection and determine how well you did and what you could have done better.

CHAPTER FIVE

LEADING IN CRISIS

When written in Chinese, the word 'crisis' is composed of two characters. One represents danger and the other represents opportunity.

- John F. Kennedy

In 1993, an elderly couple in Tacoma, Washington reported that a syringe had been found in a can of diet Pepsi. Another woman, a few miles away, reported finding a syringe in a can of Pepsi can. Suddenly, consumers all over the country seemed to be finding hypodermic syringes in cans of Pepsi. Within days, Pepsi and FDA were swamped with over 50 reports of syringe discovery from consumers in more than 20 states. What had started out as a local incident turned into a major nationwide disaster for the Pepsi brand. Sales of Pepsi took a nosedive. Craig Weatherup, President of Pepsi Co. has a huge problem on his hands. If you are Craig, what do you do?

> *At any given moment, Leaders have the power to say:*
> *This is not how the story is going to end.*
>
> – Unknown

Leaders must handle the heat for something they personally didn't do. Crisis may or may not have been caused by the leader's actions. But, they have the responsibility to handle it. Leaders have two important bottom-lines: People & Reputation. Crisis threatens reputation. Reputation takes years to build and moments to destroy. After brand, reputation is the company's most important asset. A lot of executives use the words brand and reputation interchangeably. They are not interchangeable. A company's brand image is the collective perceptions held by customers about the company's offerings. A company's reputation is the aggregate of the public's opinion about a company's external actions. Brand is customer centric, meaning that it is the perception held in the minds of the customers. On the other hand, reputation is company centric, meaning that it is perception held in the minds of a broader group of people including employees, customers, investors, regulators, journalists and local communities. Branding can make you relevant, while reputation makes you credible. Reputation is the cornerstone for building a strong, lasting brand.

When you lose your reputation, you lose trust. And, that can seriously hurt your brand and your ability to do business in the marketplace. Brands are built on broader positive traits like respect and love. Respect is earned through a combination of performance, trust and reputation. Performance is earned through quality, service, and innovation. Trust is earned though identity, reliability, sincerity, openness and security. Reputation is earned through leadership, honesty and responsibility.

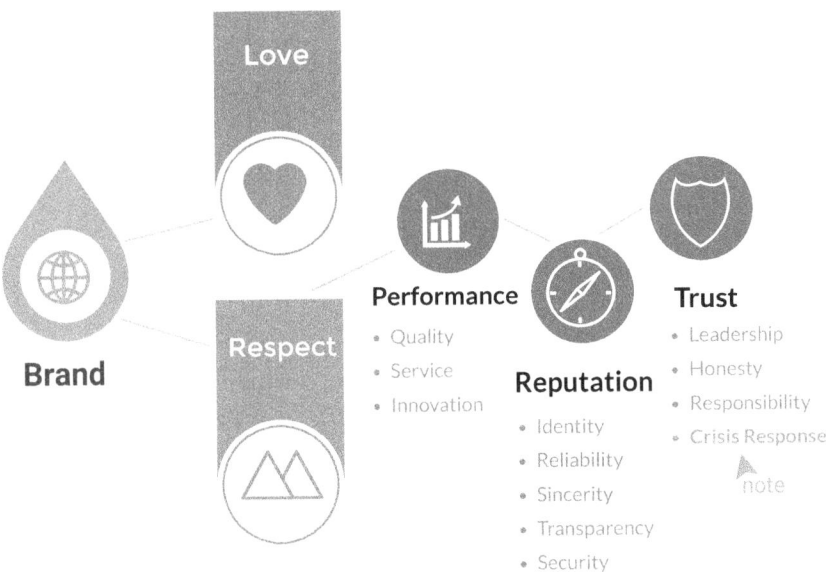

Crisis is an opportunity

Most people view crisis is a disastrous event. They are wrong. Crisis brings with it both threats and opportunities. Crisis is when you get broken. Or, you get made. Crisis is an opportunity to shape public opinion. Reputation is often shaped by how individuals and companies conduct themselves in crisis. Crisis is when you and your organization in the spotlight and people are watching closely. Problem solvers command the highest respect and attention. And, since crisis is the worst a problem can get, crisis is when people decide if you are the one they can come to when they are faced with a problem.

In 2007, the East Coast was slammed with a deadly ice storm. JetBlue was forced to cancel over 1,000 flights as its operations collapsed. Passengers were stuck in airports for nearly a week. Many of them we enraged and took their emotions to the social media. Future bookings nosedived and JetBlue had a major PR crisis on its hands. CEO David Neeleman acted swiftly to quash the uproar. The first thing he did was to instruct every employee and partner to not blame weather, even though it was clear as daylight that weather was the main cause. Neeleman appeared on television shows to offer a sincere apology rooted in empathy for the customers. He also drafted a customer's bill of rights and laid out a plan for compensating the affected customers. This PR crisis cost the company an estimated $30 million. Eventually, JetBlue recovered and is now one of the world's best-rated airlines.

WHY CRISES BLOW UP SO EASILY

No matter how much people love a brand, they subconsciously believe that for-profit businesses are inherently evil. People don't trust businesses to put values over profits. This is because businesses focus on incentives, efficiency and creation of wealth, while people focus on fairness and distribution of wealth. People are always waiting for businesses to make a mistake. It takes just a small misstep for a business. And, people do the rest. They turn it into a crisis. Social media has demoralized journalism and made crisis much easier to blow up. As a leader, everything you say and do is being watched. As a company, everything you and your employees do is being watched.

Leadership has been defined as the ability to hide your panic from others.

- Lao Tzu

LEADING IN CRISIS 96

Stakeholders

So, who is watching?

- Shareholders.
- Competitors.
- Customers, past and future.
- Employees. Yes your own employees are watching you.
- Suppliers.
- Business partners.
- Social actors.
- Media influencers.
- Experts.

- Media.
- Activists.
- Politicians.
- Regulators.
- Legislators.

In short, everybody. These are the stakeholders or constituents that businesses touch, interact with, affect, and are influenced by. Each of them have individual motivations and capabilities that can hurt us or help us during the time of crisis. Each of them can function as intermediaries for us and help us during the crisis. Accordingly, we must recognize their importance and use them to our advantage or neutralize them as needed.

Employees can be one of the most effective weapon in dealing with a crisis or they can be secretly lethal. Employees are lethal when they harbor resentment and these flare up during times of crisis where they will share key sensitive company info with outside parties.

Among the various constituents, regulators and politicians are very tricky. This is because the position taken by regulators and politicians isn't fixed. It depends on the market conditions. Both are usually very risk averse. Regulators will pounce on you especially if you have fallen out of compliance. Let me repeat myself: Regulators will never side with you if you have fallen out of compliance, even if it wasn't directly your fault. Politicians will never really openly side you even if you are a serious contributor to their campaign funds. They will however, openly oppose you if the crisis that is upon you has a massive impact and they can gather brownie points with the voting base.

If you want to be a leader who can deal with crises skillfully, you must understand how the media works. Mass media determines the issues that they think will interest the public rather than covering the issues that people should care about. The issues that receive the most attention from media become the issues that the public discusses, debates, and demands action on. Media is determining what issues and stories the public thinks about. Until the advent of social media, news journalists and celebrities played the role of influencers. In recent times, news journalists have been partly replaced by social media influencers.

Leaders must also understand the quagmire that is the legal landscape. We will cover this is in greater detail in Corporate Law but let us go over this real quick here. One on side of the legal landscape we have the statutory law which is the written law passed by the Legislators. Statutory law spells out what is permissible and not permissible in the marketplace. Our honorable courts interpret the statutory law and apply the principle of fairness to clarify ambiguities in law when deciding court cases. This sets precedents called Case law. One other side of the legal landscape, we have the Governments that oversee the executive branch. The executive branch exercises authority over regulatory agencies like Food & Drug Administration, Securities & Exchange Commission, Federal Communication Commission, etc., (that is what they are called in USA. Other countries have their equivalents, but they all basically receive orders and function the same way). In the middle of the legal landscape, we have the plaintiffs and the defendants and the legal interactions among them and the regulatory agencies is influenced by the case law and also influences the case law.

Activists and special interest groups exist at the edges of the legal landscape. They attempt to influence the politicians and the legislature to pass and amend statutory laws. Activists also have a fair amount of impact on interpretation of statutory laws by courts. Activists and interests groups have their place in the world and do a fair amount of good. But, they cause a lot of headache for leaders leading businesses. And, one day when you become a global leader, you can be sure that they will cause you a fair amount of headache for you too. Activists love to come out of the woodworks in times of crisis. They love to target companies that people care about. They like to target companies with:

- Mass market products.
- Offerings with low switching costs.
- Close substitutes in the market.
- Global operations.
- Decentralized decision hierarchy, which stops them from carefully considering external effects.

CRISIS PLANNING & PREVENTION

The key to handling a crisis comes down to one thing: already having a crisis management plan in place. Almost 90 percent of organizations remain are unprepared or significantly under-prepared for crises of any kind. What does it take to be ready? A Crisis Management Plan which is a set of documents and procedures that outlines the processes an organization will use to respond to a critical situation that would negatively impact its reputation, profitability or ability to operate. It is important to remember that crisis is not just a PR or legal issue, it concerns the whole company. Having a plan in place for crisis management is a huge part of risk management.

It takes 20 years to build a reputation and five minutes to ruin it.
If you think about that, you'll do things differently.

\- Warren Buffett

Jonathan Bernstein is a well known specialist in the field of crisis management. Bernstein maintains that the basic steps of effective crisis communications are not difficult, but they require advance work in order to minimize damage. He advises that organizational leadership often does not understand that in the absence of a proper plan:

- Operational response will break down.
- Stakeholders will not know what is happening and quickly become confused, angry, and negatively reactive.
- The organization will be perceived as inept, at best, and criminally negligent, at worst.
- The length of time required to bring full resolution to the issue will be extended, often dramatically.
- The impact to the financial bottom line and reputation will be more severe

Crisis management plan can never be one-size-fits-all. Every company is different and the plans have to be customized to the nature and intricacies of the industry. But, here is a generalized plan you can start with.

- System of Values: Crises can be of many different types. It is not possible to accurately account for all of them with changing times. The best we can do is rely something that never goes out of style. Rely on fairness and kindness. Do the right thing. Your response to

LEADING IN CRISIS 101

Crisis Managment Plan

crisis should start and with your values. When everything fails, and sometimes it will, you will be able to fall back on values. Organizational values are supremely helpful when your employees are put through a court mandated deposition. GE employees were deposed by Georgia lawyer in a wrongful death lawsuit. This crisis is covered in detail later. Values are the only sustainable way to ensure that you and your company can weather any thing that comes your way.

- Identify your important stakeholders and prioritize the order in which receive the information and responses from you. Also, set up ways in which you will reach them. Hiring PR outreach firms is a good way to reach mass market audience. If a city is working on highway redevelopment project, they will regularly use PR outreach firms to communicate with local office building administration staff regarding the upcoming route changes and closures. The admin staffs then communicates these updates to the office managers of various tenant businesses that occupy the buildings in the affected area.

- Have your ears to the ground. Use Google Alerts, Twitter and Reddit monitoring to listen for social mentions of your company and stake holders. This will help you discover problems early and nip them in the bud before they turn into crisis. Keeping your ears on the ground is an important part of crisis anticipation and listening should be especially intensified before big events like layoffs, planned recalls, etc.

- Create crisis response team by identity key employees across the company. It is important to have reps from technical department, compliance, social media, legal and human resources. Also, identify a list of reputed external consultants whom you can call upon to conduct independent investigation or offer unbiased advice. The crisis response team will be in charge of customizing the crisis management plan to suit the nature of the crisis. This team will also be in charge of assessing the effectiveness of the organizational response to crisis as well as updating the plan to perform better next time.

- Create crisis communications team. Bernstein delivers very good advice in this regard: "All stakeholders, internal and external, are just as capable of misunderstanding or misinterpreting information about your organization as the media. It's your responsibility to minimize the chance of that happening. Some chief executives are brilliant organizational leaders but not very effective in-person communicators. The decision about who should speak is made after a crisis breaks — but the pool of potential spokespersons should be identified and trained in advance". You must also train the frontline personnel who will be in touch with stake holders through the notification systems.

- Public relation should be undertaken on an ongoing basis to shape and maintain a healthy public opinion about your business. This will help bolster your communication efforts in the times of crisis.

- Prepare holding statements that will be your first line of defense when the crisis first breaks. Of course, the crisis response team should customize them to suit the nature of the crisis.

  Mild PR crisis like shipment delays, racial discrimination crisis: "We are sorry for what happened. We are working to find answers to the problem and we will not stop till we have all the answers. We promise to provide additional information as soon as we have them.

  We are here for you. If you have any questions or assistance , we are available at 24/7 at:
  Telephone:<company toll free phone>
  Email: <company email>
  Twitter: @companyhotline".

  Moderate crisis with injuries and/or financial loss "We apologies to everyone affected by this grave crisis. And send our heartfelt prayers.

  We are working to find out what happened and promise to provide updates on this crisis as soon as they become available.

  We are here for you. If you have any questions or assistance , we are available at 24/7 at:
  Telephone:<company toll free phone>
  Email: <company email>

Twitter: @companyhotline".

Extreme crisis with deaths and injuries "We apologize unconditionally for the terrible tragedy that is upon us. Our hearts go out to the victims, families and loved ones of those affected by this terrible disaster.

We working to find answers to the problem and promise to provide daily updates. We promise to do everything we can to make it right for everyone affected by this crisis.

We are here for you. If you have any questions or assistance , we are available at 24/7 at:
Telephone:<company toll free phone>
Email: <company email>
Twitter: @companyhotline".

Strict customer relations, PR and social media policy is a crucial part of having a sound crisis management plan. What happens if you don't have them in place? In 2015, Mellissa Grogan-Morgan visited the 47 King West Street restaurant in Manchester as part of her bachelorette party celebrations. They got extremely subpar treatment from what was supposed to be an upmarket restaurant. Having spent over £600 on the meal, Melissa and her friends took to facebook to criticize the restaurant on their page. A restaurant employee took control of the facebook account and responded with "The most chavviest, worst, most vile people ever to grace our restaurant. Wouldn't know fine dining if it slapped them in their ugly faces." He continued, "And 5 out of 18 of them turned up 1 hour and 10 minutes after the booking time and 'expected' fresh starters...are you having a laugh...clearly never eaten out in a decent restaurant in their lives. What absolute trash they were. We pity the groom!". The employee kept going. "Best thing ever

> Lynsey Herron — 1★ Me and a friend booked this restaurant for a hen do. When we arrived we waited for a while before being shown to our "tables" the restaurant somehow thought it acceptable to put 10 of us on one table and 8 on another, which was never outlined to us before our arrival - they said there was nothing they could do as it just wasn't possible to sit 18 on the same table despite the fact the manager (Bar... See More
> Like Comment 19 hours ago 2 Reviews
>
> 👍 3 people like this.
>
> 47 King Street West Chav cheap trash hen party!
> 19 hours ago Like
>
> 47 King Street West Turned up over an hour late. Booked for 10 then were 20. Never seen fine dining in their lives. The bottom of the barrell of Society!
> 19 hours ago Like
>
> 47 King Street West Peasants wanting something off the bill as usual!
> 19 hours ago Like
>
> Melissa Grogan-Morgan what a mature response?!

is that they won't return! Bottom of the barrel (sic)". These responses spread like wildfire as new outlets picked up and the story went viral. Eventually, the owner of the restaurant labelled the incident 'regrettable' and promised internal investigation. But, the damage to reputation had been done.

> *In time of crisis people want to know that you care,*
> *more than they care what you know*
>
> - Will Rogers, American Actor

Since you are enjoying these anecdotes so much, here is one more. In 2013, a waitress from an Applebee's restaurant in St. Louis outlet posted an unusual receipt on social media.

A Pastor had taken her some of congregation members out for a meal. Restaurant in USA charge 18% on top of the regular bill for parties larger than 5 patrons. The pastor did not like it. She wrote on the bill 'I give god 10%, why do you get 18%?' as a protest against the company's policy in regards to large-party dining. The picture of the receipt went viral news stin regard toations across the country, causing a great deal of unwanted attention for the pastor. She claimed that was told that she had brought 'embarrassment to the church and ministry'. Applebee's fired the waitress who uploaded the picture stating that it breached the pastor's privacy by including her full name. One single waiter was able to bring embarrassment to Applebee's and cause significant damage to the restaurant's reputation.

You want one more? OK, Here it is. In 2013, users on a popular discussion website 'Reddit' stumbled upon something bizarre. They noticed that one of the billboards (depicting a kettle) advertising American retailer JC Penney resembled Hitler. This observation went viral. Telegraph picked up the story and then the rest of the media outlets picked it up. Social media went viral with fun tweets and comments. No matter what anyone else says, this is a crisis because it compromises the brand integrity. A brand cannot become a joke. This is an example of a relatively milder crisis, but JC Penney handled it well. They decided that the medicine must fit the ailment. They decided to not take themselves too seriously. JC Penney engaged advertising houses to come up with equitable responses. The advertising partners delivered and soon social media saw comments and replies like, "Totally unintentional. If we had designed it to look like something, we would have gone with a snowman J". Thanks to a measured response, the crisis died down. What did we learn: In dealing with crisis, make sure that your response is appropriate and not overboard.

HANDLING THE CRISIS

Once you have a sound crisis management plan in place, navigating through crisis should be a matter of following the plan with a few changes. Again, values should guide the company during crisis because it helps provide a solid anchor that stakeholders can believe in. Remember, people don't trust businesses and that is why you must give people something they can believe in. Daniel Diermeier is a major force in the world of crisis management. He regularly advises major corporations around the world including McDonalds, J&J, FBI, UnitedHealth on how to manage their reputation and handle crises. His book 'Reputation rules' is a must read if you want to get better at handling crises. Diermeier taught me that the company's communication should address the following four areas:

- Commitment: Leaders must show up and be front and center in the crisis.

Handling Crisis

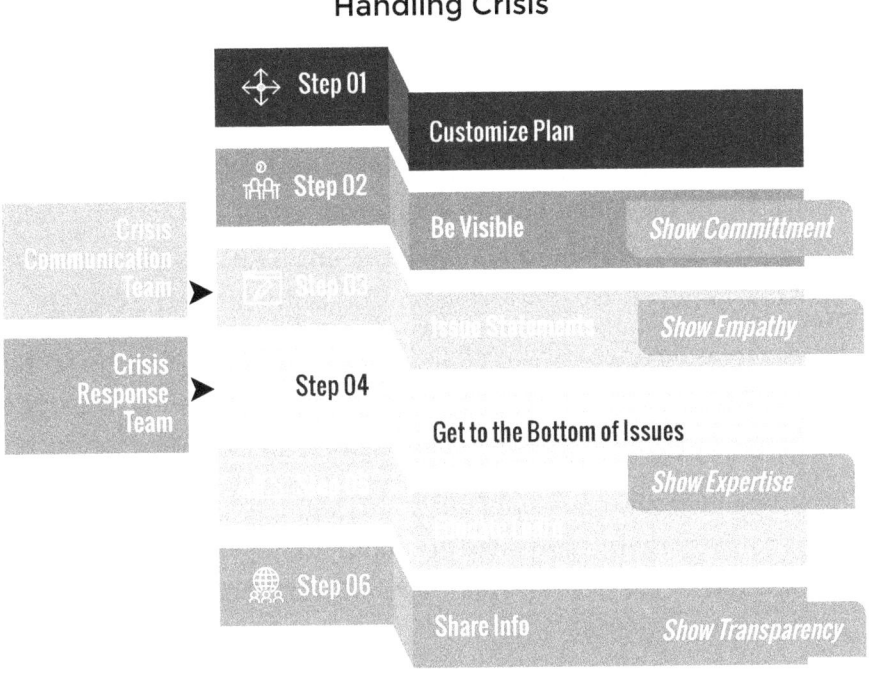

- Empathy: Most leaders don't always take ownership for disasters, but smart leaders know that successful crisis management requires starting with core values and empathy and acceptance of responsibility even if you are not fault.

- Transparency: Share information at the right time with stakeholders to earn their confidence.

- Expertise: Be humble and call on the expertise of your key employees and external consultant to help investigate the issue, collect evidence and get to the bottom of the issues. Moreover, you will personally need to understand the issues inside out and be prepared to answer the questions at a moment's notice.

Depending on the nature of the crisis, make changes to the crisis response team and the crisis communication team to include internal and external experts who can offer expertise.

- As the leader or CEO, you should make yourself extremely visible. Postpone all meetings not related to the crisis and let your family know that you will be out of pocket until this crisis is resolved. This is where you are delivering on Commitment to the crisis.

- With the assistance of the crisis communications team, you must customize the holding statements and issue the initial statements to the media. This is where you are delivering on Empathy.

- As leader, you should be in constant touch with the crisis response team to keep them motivated to deploy their expertise and get to the bottom of the issues. Ask them to reach out to you in case of any key developments.

- Share info with the stakeholders including regulator, authorities, attorney general, and take them into confidence. This is where you are delivering on Transparency .

- Depending on the crisis you will need to restructure your company for credibility, revise pay and systems, make personnel changes, make changes to control, financial and compliance systems or revise incentive structures.

What happens if you don't address all four areas. Let's find out. In 2014, Mary Barra, after working for GE Motors for 33 years, was named as the first female CEO. Eight weeks later, Lance Cooper, a Georgia attorney sued GM on behalf of the family of a woman who had died in a crash. Lance obtained thousands of pages of documents from GM and took the deposition of several GM engineers. He discovered that GE was internally aware of the issue for about a decade and that an employee lied about their awareness of the issue. Soon news broke out that there were 29 million GE cars (GE owns brands like Cadillac, Chevrolet, Buick among others) on the road with an ignition switch defect that was responsible 13 deaths and 31 crashes. Mary was summoned before the Congress and NHTSA. Along with a crushing expense that comes from such massive recalls, Mary had a major PR crisis on her hands.

Mary tackled the crisis head on. She realized that when people have lost lives, no amount of technical evidence would be enough. She appeared on national TV in front of millions of viewers and apologized personally by assuming the blame and thus, empathizing with the families and loved ones of accident victims. Her words were, "Something went very wrong…and terrible things happened." Media loved it. Bloomberg reported, "She showed a human side and that's what you have to do." New York times said, "She's owning it". Mary hired external consultants like Kenneth Feinburg to help GE decide how to compensate families of those injured by the recalled cars. She also hired external attorney Anton Valukas to help find out why GM took so long to initiate a recall of the defective cars. Mary also created reserves to compensate the families of 124 victims. Pursuant to these action, the general sentiment was that GE would become a more customer-focused company with her as the CEO than it was when GM first found out about the faulty switches. So, where did Mary fall short? Expertise. In the congressional testimony, Barbara Boxer, the Senator from California asked Barra why, during the 33 years she worked at GM prior to becoming the CEO in 2013, she never heard anything about the faulty ignition switches. After Barra failed to give a substantive answer, Boxer exclaimed to her that, "You don't know anything about anything," and that, "if this is the new GM leadership, it's pretty lacking." Mary's lack of expertise and failure to educate herself on the issue brought her embarrassment which could have been avoided with a strong focus on the expertise part of crisis response.

WHAT DO PEPSI AND CRAIG DO?

So, what did Craig do with the Pepsi syringe crisis on his hands? The first thing to do is never refute any accusations immediately and directly. Quickly denying accusations puts you in a defensive position. The best thing to do is to wait to make public announcements until you have extremely strong evidence and then be the purveyor of that evidence. And, gently persuade all parties involved to reach the conclusion. Yes, this is the persuasion technique we discussed in negotiations.

> *At any scale, Leaders are defined in moments of crisis.*
>
> **- Unknown**

Craig got to work immediately. He quickly created a crisis team consisting of specialists from different departments of the company and put the team into action. All along the way, Craig made sure that the team worked closely with FDA and made sure that any information was shared both ways ensuring complete transparency. By doing this, they took the officers from FDA into complete confidence and earned their support.

The crisis team analyzed the syringe reports and saw no logical pattern. "We were reasonably confident that this wasn't a manufacturing issue," the team said. "Canning lines are high-speed production lines in which cans are inverted upside down, shot with a blast of air or water and then [turned] right side up and filled." Since the cans are open for only nine-tenths of a second, he said, "It would be highly unlikely for one needle to find its way into a can. And it would be astronomically improbable to have numerous needles in different cans in different states, produced months apart, and then have them all somehow show up in a 48-hour period. It was absolutely ludicrous." News week later reported.

Then, Pepsi got lucky. In Aurora, Colorado, a surveillance camera at a supermarket counter caught a shopper in the act of inserting a syringe into a can of diet Pepsi. Armed with the evidence, Weatherup appeared on Channel ABC's Nightline, along with FDA official, Kessler to debunk the nationwide frenzy. Even though Pepsi had irrefutable evidence, Craig made a point to have FDA official on the Nightline show alongside him Why? Because we have discussed that people don't trust the businesses as much as they trust the governing agencies. Kessler confirmed that many of the tampering claims "could not be substantiated or verified." Craig presented the visual evidence showing a woman putting a syringe into a can of Pepsi, that proved the reports were false. Shortly thereafter, the FDA announced the first arrest on charges of filing a false report, a federal offense punishable by five years in prison and a $250,000 fine.

Before and after the show, PepsiCo also produced a series of informational videos that showed how the soda canning process worked to help provide a useful platform for people to believe that the syringe could not have been introduced during production and improve their confidence in the quality of Pepsi products.

Owing to Weatherup's leadership during the crisis and well timed coordination of the release of evidence and public announcements, the rumors gradually died down and sales began to recover in no time.

RECAP

In this chapter, we covered everything it takes to be a leader who can effectively deal with crisis. First, we looked at why crisis blow up so easily and who are the important stakeholders. Next, we looked at how to plan before a crisis happens followed by a coverage of how to handle a crisis.

ACTION ITEM

Can you think of a time you were faced with a crisis at work? Apply everything we discussed here to assess how you or your company did in that situation. Reflect on the mistakes you made (we all make mistakes… the only ones who don't make any mistakes are the ones who don't do anything) and what you could do better next time.

CHAPTER SIX

LEADERSHIP IN CORPORATE GOVERNANCE

Being powerful is like being a lady. If you have to tell people you are, you aren't!

- Margaret Thatcher

As, CEO and chairman of Nissan, Carl Ghosn was one of the most powerful and admired executives. Was. Past tense. His downfall arose from reports of three primary allegations: incorrectly reporting his compensation over a period of years, leveraging a company investment fund for personal use and inappropriately filing expense reports. A single person in charge of executing the company's vision (as CEO) as well as overseeing that the CEO's job is being done well (as chairman of the board). Of course, things are going to go wrong eventually. The concentration of power in the hands of one person, abetted by a disenfranchised or deferential board, can become a breeding ground for executive misconduct. Great leaders should have the humility to give up power, allow someone else to be the chairman and accept their challenging oversight, especially when they do not have to.

A big thing that is severely lacking in business leadership today is responsible corporate governance. And, this all comes down to leaders who do not want to give up control. Or, are secretly hungry for power. This creates an unsustainable enterprise which will eventually get dismantled by antitrust rules, taken over by activist corporate raiders or left in dust by a more innovative rival.

If your mother read about it in the Wall Street Journal, would she yell at you about it? That's the governance test used by Icahn Enterprises (Carl Celian Icahn is a corporate raider who targets companies that are not operating optimally) for the directors of the companies it invests in. The firm believes that the board of directors are there to represent shareholders, and if they are secretly representing their own interests, they become an Icahn target.

What is Responsible Corporate Governance?

The process and rules under which a company is responsibly managed on the behalf of shareholders and stakeholders. It makes companies more accountable and transparent to investors and gives them the tools to respond to stakeholder concerns. How does corporate governance differ from management? Management is about doing and execution inside the company. Governance is about oversight from outside the company.

LEADERSHIP IN CORPORATE GOVERNANCE

I have nothing but contempt for the kind of governor who is afraid, for whatever reason, to follow the course that he knows is best for the State.

- Sophocles, Greek playwright

Corporate Structure

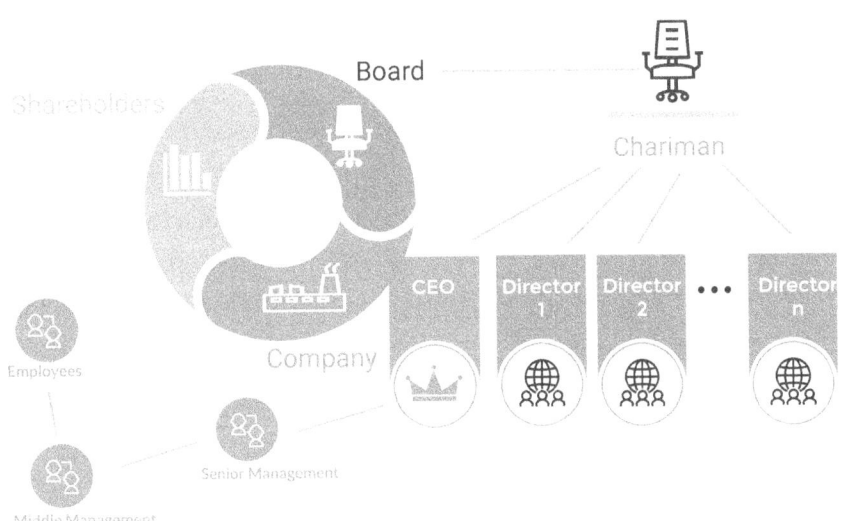

Shareholders appoint the board of directors, provide the capital, and approve the compensation for the board of directors. Board of directors appoint the CEO (and have a say in the appointment of other top executives), decide his compensation, and set the mission for the company. CEO is inside the company looking out. Board of directors are outside the company looking in. Shareholders bear the risks. They are the owners of the company. The company and the board of directors are both accountable to the shareholders. Directors are the trustee and shareholders are the beneficiaries. Proper governance ensures the division of power and establishes mechanisms to achieve accountability and transparency among stakeholders, the board of directors and management. Corporate responsibility demands that the board work to actively avoid circumstances when too much power is accumulated in an executive office that is occupied by too powerful a personality. Here is the basic corporate responsibility principle: "As the power and influence of the CEO increases, so also must the attentiveness and engagement of the board in order to assure meaningful director oversight."

Conflict of Duty and Interest in Boards

Conflict of interest and duty is a huge problem with board of directors. This is because most boards are composed of influential gazillionaires who are already on boards of other companies or are active CEO's of other companies. Active CEOs are often coveted board members because of their experience. When you consider what a CEO has to do at their own company, are they really going to be able to spend the time and effort necessary to be an effective member of the board at another company? Pretty hard to do. One way to remedy this would be to hire fewer active executives and more retired executives. Directors have a fiduciary responsibility which is the duty of loyalty. Accordingly the board must demonstrate unyielding loyalty to the company shareholders. Corporate law grants directors wide discretion when considering the interests of stakeholders. Once the duties of care are met, the courts will defer to director's "business judgment" in deciding court cases brought on by investors who lost money in the stock market because of "breach of duty" decisions made by the board. This is why most smart board members use this line before announcing decisions: "We made our decision after careful consideration of what would be in the best long-term interest of the company and its shareholders."

The "Should-be's" of a Good Board

- The responsibilities, accountabilities and agenda of the board should be defined in a document called "Board Mandate". The mandate should be available for everyone to see and it wouldn't be the worst thing if the mandate is included in the Annual report.

- The board should be composed of a right combination of executive directors, independent directors and non-independent non-executive directors to prevent one individual or a small group of individuals from dominating the board's decision making.

- A board committees may be formed to assist the board in the effective performance of its duties. There should be a formal, rigorous and transparent process for the appointment, election, induction and re-election of directors.

- There should be a formal, rigorous and transparent process for the appointment, election, induction and re-election of directors.

- The board should be responsible for risk governance and should ensure that the organization develops and executes a comprehensive and robust system of risk management. Board members should keep in mind the about the amount of risk shareholders desire help build an internal framework in the company that flags existing and potential risks. Why is this important? In 2012 JPMorgan Chase had no directors with risk expertise on the board's risk committee. This deficiency that was corrected only after Bruno Iksil, the "London Whale," caused $6 billion in trading losses. CEO, Jamie Dimon labelled this as a "Risk 101 mistake."

- The board should establish formal and transparent arrangements to appoint and maintain an appropriate relationship with the organization's auditors.

- The board should ensure that the company is compliant with applicable laws and regulations.
- Board has an obligation to the community of interest that sustains the corporation. This is in the long term interest of the corporation itself.

Sarbanes-Oxley Act to the rescue

> *I would rather be an artist than a leader. Ironically, a leader has to follow the rules.*
>
> *- Criss Jami*

In USA, the Congress passed the Sarbanes-Oxley law in 2002 in reaction to a strong of financial scandals which involved companies like Enron and WorldCom, that shook public confidence in corporate America. Enron, which back then was the seventh-largest company in America, became embroiled in a scandal over its accounting practices and eventually collapsed Subsequent investigations uncovered widespread efforts to manipulate the company's stock price. Enron executives systematically misrepresented the company's assets, hid liabilities, and overstated its earnings. Numerous Enron executives were eventually convicted of financial crimes and its accounting firm, Arthur Anderson, later went out of business.

The biggest determinant in our lives is culture, where we are born, what the environment looks like. But the second biggest determinant is probably governance, good governance or a certain kind of governance makes a huge difference in our lives.

- Nicolas Berggruen, American Businessman

The act is named after the US Senators Paul Sarbanes and Michael Oxley, who were the primary sponsors of the bill. The primary goal of the Sarbanes-Oxley Act was to recast the CEO/board dynamic away from the powerful CEO and the resultant passive board, towards more involved, independent governance. This act has had a profound impact on governance not only in USA but also in most European and Asian countries. This has been happening because many companies are global. The act is painfully elaborate, but here are some of the high level requirements of the act for companies to be compliant:

- Executives must certify that they've reviewed the financial reports, that the reports are accurate, and that the company has internal controls in place to ensure accurate financial disclosures and prevent fraud and misrepresentation.

- Companies are required to develop internal controls to ensure the accuracy of its financial reports. External auditors are required to attest to this internal control assessment as well.

- All accountants who audit public companies should be regulated by the The Public Company Accounting Oversight Board (PCAOB). Before this at, the accounts were self-regulated, much like medical professionals and lawyers currently are.

- The act makes it a crime to defraud shareholders of publicly traded companies through the filing of misleading financial reports. Fine vary form millions of dollars to years in prison. The act also criminalizes the falsification and destruction of records to impede or influence an investigation.

- The act prohibits retaliation (suspension, threatening, harassment, demotion, etc) against whistleblowers who lawfully report corporate misdeeds. The act provides a civil route for employees who are subjected to retaliation, allowing them to sue the offending employer.

All this burden of compliance comes at steep cost both financially as well as a consequent risk averse corporate decision making culture. Most companies report spending almost 1.5% of total operating expenses on total regulatory and corporate governance expenses. 75% of fortune 500 firms have a chief governance officer (usually a lawyer specialized in corporate law) and they have a team to go along with them.

RECAP

In this chapter, we explored what it takes to be a responsible leader when being part of a board of directors. We first looked at what responsible corporate governance is. Next, we covered the conflict of duty and interest that makes the company a sitting duck for angry investor lawsuits. After that, we looked at what leaders should put in place to have a good board of directors. Finally, we looked at important items leaders must be vigilant of to be complaint with Sarbanes-Oxley Act when functioning with boards of public companies.

ACTION ITEM

If you work for a public company or an organization that has a board of directors, attempt to learn everything about this board, who serves on it, what other companies these directors are involved with, and how involved these directors are in the strategic direction, policy making and oversight of the company.

CHAPTER SEVEN

MASTERING LEGAL QUAGMIRE: BUSINESS LAW

Litigation is the basic legal right which guarantees every corporation its decade in court.

- David Porter

In a 1996, Pepsi launched a marketing campaign advertising that points that could be redeemed for Pepsi stuff like t-shirts, hats, etc. Pepsi then ran several television commercials promoting the campaign. At the end of one such commercial a student was portrayed showing up to school in his new Harrier jet and the words "7,000,000 points" flashing across the TV screen. Mr. Leonard, age 24, of Miami-Dade County Florida collected 15 Pepsi Points and together with a check in the amount of $699,998.50 (for 6,999,985 additional points) forwarded a request to redeem the Harrier jet worth roughly $23 million. Pepsi refused to honor the request saying it was a joke. Mr. Leonard filed suit against

Pepsi. If you were the judge presiding this case, what would you do? Take a moment. US District Judge Kimba Wood sided with Pepsi saying, "No objective person could reasonably have concluded that the commercial actually offered consumers a Harrier jet." Judge went further to say, "But the court's observations make for a great source of deadpan humor, with comments such as, "The callow youth featured in the commercial is a highly improbable pilot, "one who could barely be trusted with the keys to his parents' car, much less the prize aircraft of the United States Marine Corps."

Competent leaders must be extremely well-versed with law because every business proposal, contract and transaction happens in the arena of law. Knowledge of the law is essential to

- Ensure that contracts are drafted correctly to ensure it will be easy yo enforce them
- To know the boundaries of law so that u know how much to push them
- Prevent lawyers from taking you for a ride and over-bill you.
- Deal with exceptions like lawsuits. Whether you are the owner of the company or the manager of a department, you will be the one would have to deal with exceptions like issues, lawsuit, lawsuits, mediation, etc.
- Need to know what to do to avoid lawsuits.

We can spend the rest of our life learning about law and it wouldn't enough simply because there is so much to know. So, my goal here is to equip you with enough knowledge to be skilled in matters of handling everyday business. The legal systems of the world are generally based on one of the following systems:

- Civil law
- Common law
- Religious law
- Statutory law

Legal systems are designed to keep the populace in check. And, even though we speak different languages and eat different foods, people everywhere are essentially the same. That is the reason why laws and the legal systems vary in nuances in different countries, but at a macro level, they are pretty much the same. I am covering the US legal system here, but you must read up on how the legal system is structured in your beloved country. Let's go.

The Legal System

The US Federal system of government is built upon the US constitutions which ensures separation of powers by having three separate branches of government: Legislative, Executive and Judicial.

- The Legislative branch or the Congress makes the law where members draft and sponsor a bill. House Action Committee studies, researches and revises the bill and then returns it to the house for floor vote. Once the bill is signed by both Chambers of the Congress: the House of Representatives and the Senate, it is sent to the President for his signature.
- The Executive branch enforces the law through regulatory agencies like Food and Drug Administration, Securities and Exchange Com-

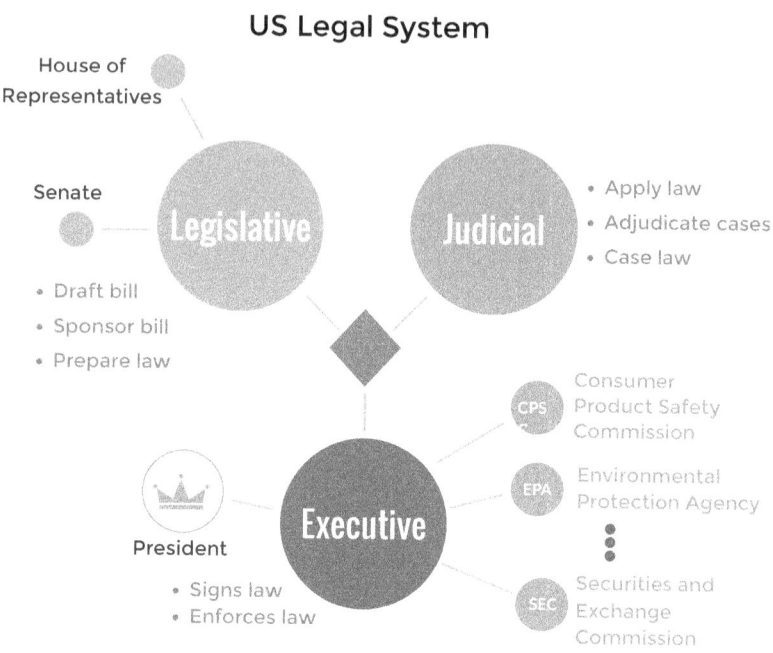

mission, Environmental Protection Agency, Federal Energy Regulatory Commission to name a few. The legislature and the President, who is the head of the executive branch, pass statute giving regulatory agencies the authority to regulate. The regulatory agencies make the regulations through a due process called Administrative Procedures Act(APA) that gives individuals and businesses due legal rights in the process of formation of rules. Basically, the agencies propose the regulations and provide the "notice of proposed rule-making" in the *Federal Register,* as well as in relevant industry or trade publications. Congressional Review Act enacted in 1996 requires agencies to submit reports to the House of Representatives, the Senate, and the Comptroller General regarding any new rule covered by the CRA. Finally, the public is allowed to submit comments on them and the agencies must respond in a reasonable manner before the rules can be presented for Signature to the President.

- The Judicial branch interprets the laws and regulation and applies principles of fairness and commonsense to decide court cases. As common law courts, US courts have inherited the principle of *stare decisis*. American judges, like common law judges elsewhere, not only apply the law, they also make the law, to the extent that their decisions in the cases before them become precedent for decisions in future cases. Courts are frequently called upon to review the actions of legislature and executive branch to decide if the law or regulation is constitutional.

US Courts System

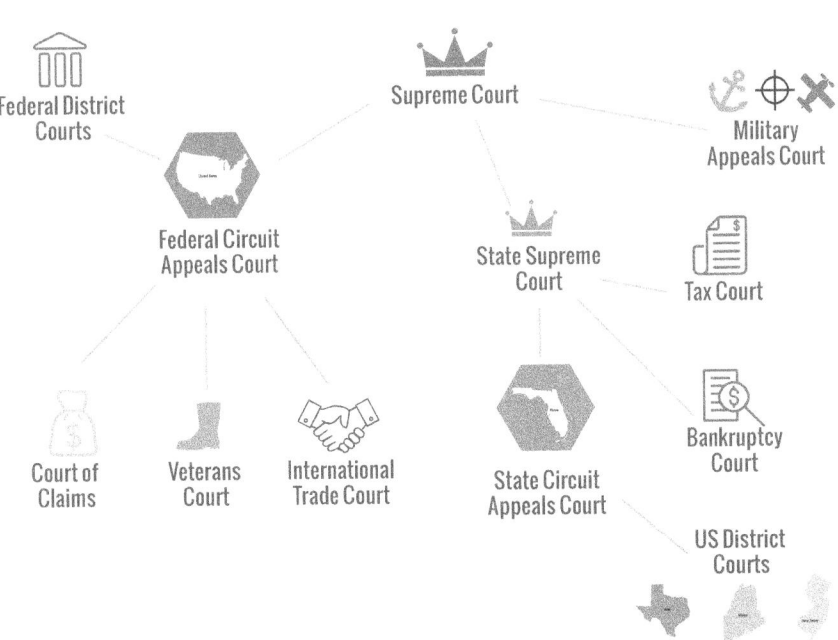

There are more lawyers in just Washington, DC than in all of Japan. They've got about as many lawyers as we have sumo-wrestlers.

- Lee Iacocca, Auto Industry Executive

The US legal system is structured as a dual system of law: the federal law and the state law with a dual system of courts: federal courts and the state courts. There are many different types of laws that apply to commerce: Common law, contract law, tort law, employment law, labor laws, bankruptcy law, tax law, etc. Many of these laws emerge from the Uniform Law which has been adopted by most states in USA. For example, the state contract law is based on the Uniform Commercial Code. These laws provide the stability and predictability upon which business and individuals can rely on to reduce their risks in conducting business and reliably fallback on for remedy. In many cases, juries are called upon to help settle lawsuit. Juries are usually 12 citizens selected from tax or voter records. Juries tend to favor individuals over businesses and locals over outsiders.

I have come to the conclusion that one useless man is called a disgrace, two men are called a law firm, and three or more become a Congress.

- John Adams Character in the Play "1776"

Challenging Laws & Regulation

Skilled leaders must use their team and resources to excel at business while staying within the bounds of laws and regulations. How does regulation differ from law? Let us look at this using the example of

Challenging Regulation

parking under a "No Parking" sign. Usually, a parking enforcement officer writes a parking ticket, and you can either pay the fine or appear before the judge. If a regulatory agency like EPA wrote the rules for parking violations, the officer would first have to determine if there were sufficient legal parking available at a reasonable cost and at a reasonable distance, and would then have to stand by the car and wait until the owner showed up so that he could negotiate a settlement agreement. Regulations are more fluid than law. Leaders can use the legal system to their advantage by erecting regulation and laws against others through lobbying or by challenging regulations that have been erected against them.

Lobbying must be used strategically by leaders to help enact regulation and laws through lobbying to create barriers to entry for competitors.

Lobbying is a lot like teaching: You, a subject matter expert, and your lobbying consultant (your bridge to the lawmakers) use your personal stories to educate individuals who are pretty clueless about your subject. You just happen to be talking to lawmakers, congressional committees, the courts, and top government officials about policy, instead of third graders about division and multiplication. Influential lobbying consultants or 'Lobbyists' can be mostly found working at lobbying firms. William & Jensen, Ernst & Young, Ogilvy Relations are some major lobbying firms. Most businesses can expect to spend anywhere form $10k to $1 million on lobbying efforts per year. A group called OpenSecrets lists major lobbying firms and the amount companies that have spent with these lobbying firms to advance their interests. In certain situations, for example, if you are a nonprofit that receives federal grant funding, be careful during lobbying because the Internal Revenue Code prohibits what you can say and do during lobbying.

> *Where there is a will there is a lawsuit.*
>
> \- Addison Mizner, 19th Century Architect

They must also **challenge regulations** that have been erected as barriers against them by others. Here are the common arguments you can use to challenge regulations against you:

- Agency's interpretation is unconstitutional because it violates the commerce clause, free speech, etc.
- Agency misinterpreted the statue from the legislature

- Agency did not follow proper procedures when forming the regulation. For example, they might not have given enough notice or taken into account certain comments.
- Agency's conclusions regarding the need for this regulation are arbitrary and non sensical.
- Agency has not provided substantial evidence to document my violation of the regulation.

When Congress passed the Family Smoking Prevention and Tobacco Control Act in 2009, FDA issued regulations that banned the used of colors and graphics on cigarette packaging in order to reduce the attraction of cigarettes to children. I am not against tobacco or not it. But, I have to side here with FDA for one thing. We must do everything to protect our children. Big Tobacco realized that the side effect of this would be reduced sales to adults.The army of lawyers at big tobacco got the Federal Appeals court to strike down this regulation on grounds that it was unconstitutional because it violated the first amendment right to free speech of tobacco companies.

Contract Formation

Contract law is the area of law that governs making contracts, carrying them out and providing a fair remedy when there is a breach. Contract law is provided by Article 2 of Uniform Commercial Code and the warranty act. A valid contract should have four parts:

- Offer made by one party.
- Acceptance by another party.
- Each party should give up something. This is called Bargained for Consideration.

Contract Formation

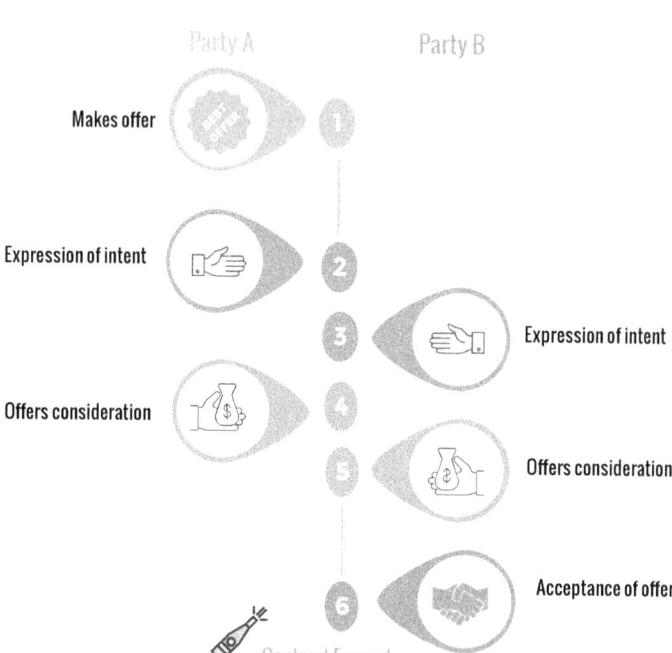

- Both parties must have mutual intent to be bound by the contract.

It is very important to be clear about when an enforceable contract is formed.

If Jack tells Suzy, "I will be away at the music festival for a week. If you watch my horse here while I am away, and call me if anyone tries to steak him I will give you $1000". Suzy watches the horse while Jack is away. Jack returns and refuses to pay Suzy because he believes that nobody tried to steal the horse since he got no call from Suzy, so he doesn't owe Suzy any money. What do you think? If they went to court, Jack would be ordered to pay Suzy $1000 because $1000 has been bargained for Suzy's time to watch the horse and the makes a contract.

Contracts can be implied. If you walk into a restaurant and order a meal, you are under enforceable contract to pay for it. If you go to a dentist and get a cleaning done, you are under enforceable contract to pay for it. Imagine having to wait for the dentist to call his lawyer, get a contract prepared that says that you will pay the dentist if he cleans your teeth. Contracts make life easier because of the reasonable, implied nature. Suppose, you run a restaurant with a landscaped yard and have a lawn guy, Julio who comes every week to cut the grass in exchange for $50 cash. If you hire another lawn guy Jose to do the same thing, you are obligated to inform Julio that you do not need his services anymore. Otherwise, if Julio shows up at the usual time and day of the week and starts working on the lawn, you will owe him money as part of an implied enforceable contract.

Contracts can be formed with a unilateral promise (promise for an action). If party A says to party B, "If you build me a greenhouse, I'll pay you $50k." Party B doesn't have to say anything. They could order materials and show up at the job-site (being substantial performance) to start building the greenhouse and that is when the contract would be formed.

Contracts can be formed with a bilateral promise (promise for a promise). If party B says, "I promise to build you a greenhouse if you promise to pay me $50k". Party A says, " It's a deal". Contract is formed.

However, if party A says, "I promise to pay $50k to the first person who builds me a greenhouse within a week". If party B says, "It's a deal", contract is not formed. If party B builds the greenhouse within a week, contract is formed. I know this sounds confusing. But, that is the legality of the law.

Contracts can be formed with an offer. As soon as you give someone an offer, you give them the right to bind you to a contract. Suppose party B says to party A, "I offer to build you a greenhouse with a week if you pay me $50k". If party A says, "We accept your offer. But, you need to complete it within 3 days. Kindly confirm." This implies that no contract has been formed since party A has rejected the offer. In contrast, if party A says, "We accept your offer. Can you finish the greenhouse in 3 days?", a contract has been formed because the A accepted the offer.

The medium of communication for contract formation could be an in person conversation, a phone call, email, chat or snail mail. The difference with snail mail is that contracts are formed when person accepting the offer dispatches the offer acceptance to the other party. This is also the reason that the person who made the offer in the first place cannot revoke the offer once the other party has dispatched the offer acceptance in the mail. Regard that advertisements, price charts, and catalogs are not offers, but instead are requests for offers or invitations to bargain or negotiate.

The original concept of a contract is a *bargained-for* exchange of consideration. In contrast, a "contract of adhesion" is a form of contract in which the party being asked to sign it has no choice but to take it or leave it. They're always unfair because there's no bargaining power. That is the very definition of a contract of adhesion. Courts supposedly look unfavorably on contracts of adhesion, but unless they involve a service on which the public depends (such as medical services or public education), they're upheld.

Did you know that every time you click "Accept" on an online click-thru agreement, you've bound yourself to a legal contract? It is not necessary that you should have read the fine print. You just have to have navigated past it to get to a point where your acceptance is recorded.

> *I learned law so well, the day I graduated I sued the college, won the case, and got my tuition back.*
>
> **- Fred Allen, Iconic American Comic**

There is an exception to the need for consideration in contract formations. This exception is called the Promissory Estoppel. The elements of promissory estoppel determine whether the remedies that are available to the injured party are equitable, or fair. This means that the court has discretion in deciding how best to make the situation right. Say, Mark loves a local restaurant that serves delectable Chinese food. Mark strikes up a conversation with the owner, gets him excited about opening a Japanese food extension in the vacant premises next door and promise to finance half of the expenses of the extension for $50K. A month later, Mark visits the restaurant and lets the owner know that he has changed you mind. Unfortunately, the owner has already rented the vacant premises and bought furnitures, plates and other times. If the owner went to court, would Mark have to pay $50k to the owner? Yes. Because, the owner relied on Mark's promise and undertook actions that he would not have taken otherwise. In this situation, there is no way to ensure justice to the owner without enforcing the promise.

Since, court judgements create precedents for cases that come after it, contracts should not be against public interest and should not be unconscionable for them to be iron clad.

As an example, it is common for employers to have employees working on sensitive technology sign non compete agreements if they leave the company. Most non competes are non enforceable because they are unduly restrictive or do not specify the required elements in full. For a non-compete agreement to be enforceable, it should be reasonable in the following elements:

- Time: specify the time for which the restriction applies. Generally 1-3 years.
- Jurisdictional boundaries: specify the geographic areas in which the restriction applies
- Scope: specify the nature of business activities in which the employee is forbidden to engage.

Remember, if someone gets you to sign a severely unconscionable contract by applying due stress or by coercion, that contract will not be enforceable.

Companies frequently license IP and patents from each other. So I wanted to cover a contract interpretation which has been the subject of wide dispute in case law. When entering into a contract for licensing be sure to define the scope of licensing and whether the company to which you are licensing is allowed to license the stuff to another company. Mostly, the lawyers will draft the agreements. But, look for this clause. Because, lawyers make mistakes so often that it will blow your mind.

Another thing to be wary off is the presence of ambiguous terms in the contract. Mostly if there are ambiguous terms in the contract, then the interpretation of those terms would be against the party which drafted the document. This is called 'Rule against drafter'. Because businesses, or their lawyers, usually draft the contract when they were working with employees customers or other smaller businesses, this rule works against the them. How do you protect against this? Here is the clause that should add to the contract: "Each party has cooperated in the drafting and preparation of this contract. In the event any construction needs to be made regarding the terms in this contract, the same shall not be construed against any party on the basis that the party was the scrivener (drafter)."

If a written contract seems to be complete in all terms no outside evidence should be allowed for the jury. This is called the Parol evidence rule. Liberal judges love to ignore the parole evidence rule to favor individuals over businesses. How to protect against this? Include this in the contract: "This agreement constitutes the entire agreement between the parties with respect to this matter and it supersedes and replaces all prior understandings or agreements written or otherwise."

Contract Modification

Modification of an existing contract requires new consideration for the modified contract to be enforceable. Imagine that SummerKidsCamp had a contract for $20k with CoolACGuys to perform enhancement maintenance on April 25 for their AC system to accommodate the increased number of kids expected on May 1 when school is out and summer starts. On April 24, one day before the slated maintenance date, CoolACGuys demands $30k to perform the enhancement maintenance. SummerKidsCamp agrees in writing but only pays $20k after CoolACGuys is done. If they went to court, who would prevail? SummerKidsCamp. Why? Because, CoolACGuys were under an existing enforceable contract to perform the enhancement maintenance. Accordingly, the work performed by CoolACGuys fell under the pre-existing duty rule established by the previous contract. The new contract in which SummerKidsCamp promised an extra $10k to CoolACGuys is not supported by new consideration. The exception would be the case where a component required for the maintenance is not available locally and has to be air-shipped for $10k from Europe. In this case, the law of unforeseen circumstances applies and CoolACGuys would be entitled to the extra $10k.

Contract Remedies for breach

Life is unfair and so is law. Jury awards are businesses are often large. The goal of this section is to understand what remedies are available for breach and how to limit them when these is going against you. There are two forms of monetary damages available:

- Expectation damages which aim to provide the amount or equivalent the prevailing party would have if the contract had been performed.
- Consequential damages which aim to provide for the amount or equivalent that the party in breach had reason to foresee during contract formation.

How do you limit consequential damages? Be sure to include this clause in the contract: "Neither Seller nor Purchaser shall have any liability to any other party for consequential damages, special damages, incidental damages, indirect damages, punitive damages, multiple of earnings, diminution in value or lost profits." On the other hand, if you, as an individual, are forming a contract with a business, you want to make sure that this clause is as ambiguous as possible, so that it is not fully enforceable and subject to jury interpretation. Businesses will frequently include a total limit on damages by saying something along the lines of: "Limitation of liability: The total dollar liability of either party under the agreement or otherwise shall be limited to $1500." Finally, remember that even if you manage to sneak an unreasonably large liquidated damages clause in the contract, it would be enforceable in court on grounds of being unconscionable or against fair public policy.

Uniform Commercial Code Article 2

UCC Article 2 is very important considering how much it governs the sales of goods and services in everyday life. It applies to sale of good, sales of goods and services, and does not apply to sales of only services. For most sales transactions, it provides the default basis and overcomes the issues of contract formation. It imposes a higher standard of conduct on merchants by providing a lot of default protection of buyers of goods and services. If you receive a written offer from another company in which they are offering to sell you their used delivery trucks, remember that their offer is irrevocable and is open for 3 months by default (or for whatever smaller time frame, if they specified one) unless they call you and revoke the offer before the time frame is over. After 3 months, the offer is automatically revoked unless you do one of the three things:

- Accepted the offer
- Pay some sort of consideration to keep the option open.
- Commence performance specified in the offer and notify them within a reasonable amount of time that the performance has commenced. Commence could be anything like depositing money in an escrow account.

UCC Article 2 has a lot of bearing on the warranty of title. It clarifies that a seller of goods cannot transfer a title to a buyer any better than the title the seller has. Also, the seller is liable for breach of sale contract even if they did not know about the title defect. Accordingly, to protect yourself, the following disclaimers should be included if you are selling goods that you procured from somebody else: "Seller does not warrant the title".

Titles are voided by theft. Suppose that C steals A's car and sells it to a local used car dealer, who in turn sells it to B. A will be recover the car from B. However, B will have an enforceable claim against the used card dealer even if the used car dealer was innocent. In contrast, if C had given a bad check to A in order to get the car and then sold it to the used car dealer, A would not be able to recover the car from B. A, however, would have a claim against C.

Titles are also voided by entrustment to a merchant who deals in those kind of goods. Suppose that A sends his car to local dealership for repairs. the local dealership repairs the card, but accidentally sells it to B. You will not be able to recover the car from B. B will have a good title to the car. You, however, will have a solid claim against the local dealership.

A lawyer will do anything to win a case, sometimes he will even tell the truth.

- Patrick Murray, Actor

You are, in most probability, very familiar with implied warranty of merchantability and fitness of purpose. This is the sort of warranty that allows you to have a claim against the dealership and the carmakers, should your headlights malfunction and you drive into a tree at night.

All of this is provided by UCC Article 2. Such warranties can be disclaimed by:

- Using 'As Is' language.
- Buyers's inspection or refusal to inspect, if the inspection would have revealed the problem in question

Consequential damages resulting form warranty action can be limited by including the following clause in the purchase agreement. "We do not accept liability for consequential or incidental damages. Our liability is limited to the amount you paid for the product"

Frivolous lawsuits

If you follow these lesson here well and are not too unlucky in life, immeasurable success will be your way. And, with success will come money. And, with money will come people who will want to take it away from you by way of frivolous lawsuits. Let us close the section with two mildly comical cases.

Richard Overton sued Anheuser-Busch for allegedly violating Michigan's pricing and advertising act stating that the brewing company placed ads containing images of beautiful women and tropical settings. The ads were deceptive and misleading because they implied that a person's fantasies could become reality. They also enticed the Overton and other members of the public to drink the company's products knowing fully well that alcohol is potentially dangerous as they could lead to addiction and other health problems. Overton sought more than $10,000 in damages for physical and mental injury, emotional distress, and financial loss. The court ruled in favor of Anheiser-Busch by saying that images in the ads didn't constitute fraud but were simply puffing. It also stated that the brewery had no duty to warn the plaintiff since the risks of alcoholic beverages are widely known.

Ok, One more. If you've ever been irritated by a loud neighbors playing music on full volume, you have the Hollywood Silver Fox Farms to thank for the fact that you're on the right side of law. Mr. Emmett did like his neighbors who were the owners of the Hollywood Silver Fox Farm. The farm's business was breeding silver foxes for the fur industry. Silver foxes are notoriously sensitive creatures are likely to miscarry if disturbed when pregnant. Emmett had his family make loud gun fire noises repeatedly in order to upset the foxes. It worked and the farms suffered sizable losses in population of silver foxes. They sued Emmet. Emmett defended his actions by saying that he had the right to use his land in a reasonable manner. But the court ruled that no one has "the absolute right to create noises upon his own land, because any right which the law gives him is qualified by the condition that it must not be exercised to the nuisance of his neighbors". I love loud music sometimes, but thank heavens for that judgment.

RECAP

In this chapter, we morphed into legally well-informed leaders by first looking at the US Legal System and then understanding how to laws and regulations are made and how to challenge them strategically. Next, we explored how legal contract are formed, hoot modify them so that they are enforceable and what the remedies are in case of breach. Finally, we looked at Uniform Commercial Code Article 2 and some frivolous lawsuit.

ACTION ITEM

Familiarize yourself with the laws of your land or your state and the laws and eminent cases related to the specific business you are in. Almost no one does this. But, if you do it, you will be extremely well equipped to handle legal matters in your business of for your company.

APPENDIX

MANAGEMENT DISCIPLINES

Management disciplines are areas and functions that combine synergistically to help further the company's mission. These are areas of practice that your employees specialize in. Here is a brief explanation of the various disciplines.

Marketing Management is the art and science of creating compelling offerings that align with the company's Vision and then convincing the correct subset of the target market why they should choose your products over your competitors.

Marketing Strategy helps us develop an effective plan of action to convince consumers why they should pay for your product or service and not those of your competitors.

Marketing Tactics involves making your offering available and visible to your customers in a way that rhymes with your brand positioning. Tactics include: **Advertising & Communications** which is the process of reaching and persuading the defined set of target market to prefer the company's product or service over the competitors, **Branding** which is the long-term plan for the development of a successful brand that embodies the company's vision, **Digital marketing**, and **Sales**.

Accounting is the systematic recording and reporting of financial transactions pertaining to a business.

Financial Reporting Systems disclose an organization's financial status to management, investors, and the government.

Managerial Finance is the science of planning the distribution of a company's assets.

International Finance deals with monetary interactions between two countries.

Financial Management is practice of finance with a long term view considering the *strategic* goals of the enterprise. There are three types of financial management: capital budgeting, capital structure, and working capital management.

Operations Management is the science of planning, organizing, coordinating, and controlling all the resources involved in creation of goods and services.

Strategic Decisions in Operations is the science of optimization of specific areas that affect resources involved in creation of goods and services.

Statistical Decision Analysis is the science of using statistical techniques to analyze strategic and tactical decisions.

Managerial Economics is the application of principles of economics to decision making.

Macroeconomics is the study of behavior, performance and influence of regional, national and global economies on the business.

Economics of Competition is the understanding of effects that the science of economics has on the competitive landscape.

Leadership and Organizations involves understanding the principles behind effective leadership and how to use these principles to manage organizations at any scale.

Executive Leadership helps you understand the things you must get right to properly lead a global company.

Crisis Management involves understanding how to deal with disruptive and unexpected events that threatens the organization or its stakeholders.

Strategic Negotiations help understand the negotiation techniques for handling counterparts from different cultural backgrounds at the bargaining table.

Ethics & Executive Leadership involves understanding the importance of ethical beliefs, dignity and social values to become an effective leader.

Mergers & Acquisitions involves understanding the process by which parties consolidate or distribute assets through various types of financial transactions.

Corporate Law helps get a finer understanding of company and contract law and it application to the stages in the life cycle of the corporation

Corporate Governance involves the mechanisms, relations, and processes by which a corporation is controlled and directed to balance the interests of the stakeholders.

CORPORATE ROADMAP FOR IKEA

Corporate Roadmap for IKEA

1 Purpose

To create a better everyday life for the many people

2 Values

IKEA culture reflects Swedish roots coming from Småland in southern Sweden. People living here are hard-working, down-to-earth, help each other and live in a close contact with nature around. These aspects are translated into IKEA values which form the basics of IKEA culture. "We believe that every individual has something valuable to offer and we strive to have the same values in the way we work. Our values revolve around togetherness, caring, simplicity, give and take responsibility, lead by example, and caring for people and planet."

3 Vision

Offer a wide range of well-designed, functional, affordable products for use at home (Where Ikea wants to be in the future)

4 Mission

Offer a wide range of well-designed, functional home furnishing products at prices so low that as many people as possible will be able to afford them. (What is Ikea doing now to realize its mission)

5 Goals

To realize the mission of well-designed, functional: Customize Ikea products to the needs of local markets. To realize the mission of as many people as possible: Make Ikea products available to more markets in the world. Open 200 more stores in the USA, open 10 stores over the next 5 years in India, etc.

Corporate Roadmap for IKEA (continued)

Strategy

"We have taken the straightforward approach to the furniture business, by starting with developing furniture with the price tag in mind. This is the IKEA way, to maximize the use of raw materials in order to fulfill people's needs and preferences by offering quality products at an affordable price.

"Ikea strategy differs in different markets. For example: In Europe: Good quality stylish product. Aimed at lower middle class as functional products. In China: Modifications to products to suit the Chinese apartment sizes. Aimed at middle class as aspirational products.

Tactics

- Design furnitures so that they can be assembled by the customer easily. Increases customer value proposition without hurting margins.
- Design durable furniture so that it removes the biggest anxiety related to buying furniture: "Will it last?"
- Price it low, but not too cheap, so that it removes the next set of anxiety: "Am I paying too much?" or "Am I buying cheap junk?"
- Source raw materials locally. Open stores near major highway intersections so that they are accessible to a wider geography of audience.
- Oddly naming the products like Bjorkas, Slojda and Klunsa to spark intrigue and set apart the Ikea brand and functional value proposition from other furnishing outfits. Reduces marketing cost and improves value proportion.

Implementation & Control

Ikea is a $30 billion enterprise with 139,000 employees. These are way too many to list.

BLANK ROADMAP TEMPLATE

APPENDIX 154

Blank Roadmap template
Be extremely specific and to the point

1 PURPOSE — Reason for existence

2 VALUES — Ideals in life

3 VISION — Where you want to be in future

4 MISSION — What will you do now to realize your vision

5 GOAL — Defined target you need to hit. How much and by when.

6 STRATEGY — What will you do to achieve the goal

7 TACTICS — Plan of action in few lines. How? Who? When? Where?

8 IMPLEMENTATION — Execution results

9 CONTROL — Results & Feedback

APPENDIX 155

ABOUT MYSELF

My name is Ritesh Chaube, and I was fortunate to attend The Kellogg School of Management at NorthWestern University. My academic background is in Engineering and starting and growing companies is my professional passion.

My style of writing does not fit in the regular publishing mold. I really don't understand what happens to people when they are writing. Smart, reasonable people who are pretty good at communicating and are funny in social interactions turn into robots as soon as they start writing. They don't write like they speak. It is like a cover comes over them. They start sounding boring. Maybe, they are forced to listen to the editors at these publishing companies. Editors who don't get it. I don't know what it is. Personally, I love to use day-to-day conversational terms like "shitty," "sucks," and "blows" in writing as if I am speaking to my readers.

I am fascinated with the latest research that happens in the field of management and how this latest research can be combined with industrial learnings and experience and applied to solve everyday problems.

I am obsessed with making all these things simple to understand and bringing it within the reach of professionals everywhere. With every edition, I plan to keep this book updated with the latest in the field of management, all with the solid foundational base that comes from attending the #1 Business School for Marketing in the World.

TELL ME HOW I DID

Hi,

I personally read every review and give utmost importance to feedback and reviews in choosing how to keep this work updated with latest material, research, and real business application. That is the only way to get better. To listen to the voice of your true readers.

So, if you have a chance, please write an honest review on Amazon, B&N, GoodReads, or wherever else you bought this book.

These books will be eventually converted into videos and classroom courses for individuals in upcoming countries that don't have access to high quality education. Help shape the way management is taught and learned in future.

Many Thanks!

- **Ritesh Chaube**

IN CLOSING

Thank you for sticking with me through these chapters and enduring my unusual sense of humor. Thank you for staying awake and staying the course in discovering the latest in Effective Leadership and the central importance it holds in running any business. I hope the occasional immature language mixed with quotes and fascinating facts kept you inspired and engaged.

We learned valuable lessons along the way about applying Visionary Leadership thought techniques to develop a Purpose, develop a Value system and then combining the Purpose and the Values to define a Mission. Finally, we looked at how to communicate the mission to the organization and build a strong enterprise through leadership in action. Next, we delved deeply into the art and science of negotiations and understood how indispensable effective negotiation techniques are to any leader. Then, we looked at what leaders must systematically do in moments of crisis. Finally, we covered how to lead effectively in governing a company and using our understanding of the legal system to navigate the business landscape.

If you miss the crude humor, come back and read these chapters again. All these idea will resonate resoundingly the second time around and light bulbs will come alive in your heads as you make the connections about how visionary leadership pulls the entire company together to help fulfill the corporate purpose.

IN CLOSING

Master everything we have covered here. Then, apply these kick-butt skills at work or business. Work smart and execute ruthlessly. You will be able to make a huge difference. People will find it hard to argue with the real results you will produce. Your impact will be undeniable and people will take notice. Rich rewards await.

I wrote this book for people like you and me, and I cannot wait to see what you will do with it.

Onwards!

- Ritesh Chaube

Share your stories at: 200kMBA.com/leadership/feedback

P.S.: This unusual tradition of exceptional management material fused with a side of delectable humor and urban speak continues in the next one in the series titled, *"Everything I learned at $200,000 MBA about Finance"*. Stay tuned.

www.ingramcontent.com/pod-product-compliance
Lightning Source LLC
Chambersburg PA
CBHW051059160426
43193CB00010B/1240